By Viktor E. Frankl

THE UNCONSCIOUS GOD

Psychotherapy and Theology

VIKTOR E. FRANKL

SIMON AND SCHUSTER | NEW YORK

To my sister

Published by Simon and Schuster
Rockefeller Center, 630 Fifth Avenue
New York, New York 10020
Designed by Edith Fowler
Manufactured in the United States of America
1   2   3   4   5   6   7   8   9   10

Library of Congress Cataloging in Publication Data

Frankl, Viktor Emil.
  The unconscious God.

  Translation of Der unbewusste Gott.
  Bibliography: p.
    1. Psychiatry and religion. 2. Psychotherapy. 3. Logo-
therapy. I. Title. [DNLM: 1. Psychotherapy. 2. Religion and
psychology. WM420 F831]
RC480.5.F73613   616.8'914   75-22137
ISBN 0-671-22099-3

Acknowledgments

I am indebted to the late Phil Flayderman for initiating the English translation of this book while still my editor at Washington Square Press. I also owe to his initiative and insistence the publication of a paperback edition of *Man's Search for Meaning*.

Further, I am indebted to F. Toby Weiss, who stayed in Vienna on a Fulbright fellowship granted to him in order to study logotherapy. Without his assistance—based on a unique capacity always to understand in depth what I intended to say at a given point—I could never have succeeded in bringing about this translation of my book.

Last but not least, the expression of my gratitude is extended to my wife, who typed the manuscript tirelessly, as she has almost all my other books, both German and English.

Viktor E. Frankl

Preface

The material in this book is drawn from a lecture I gave shortly after World War II, at the invitation of a small club of Viennese intellectuals. My audience was composed of no more than a dozen listeners. In 1947 the lecture was published as a book in German. It is only now, twenty-eight years after its original publication, that the book appears in an English translation. (Spanish, Dutch, Japanese and Swedish editions were published rather long before now, and a French version is on press.)

Considering the time that has elapsed since the first edition—more than a quarter of a century—it might be understood that I no longer am in a position to subscribe fully to each and every word as it was printed in 1947. My thinking has developed considerably in the meantime—developed and, I hope, also matured.

To be sure, some of the changes have been implemented in the present edition by slightly altering certain passages. However, I have deliberately refrained from major alterations of the text because, of my twenty books, this is the most organized and systematized one, and it would have been a pity to destroy the cohesive structure of this piece of work by interspersing too much of the material that might have accrued in the meantime.

All the more, I welcomed the alternative which my publishers, Simon and Schuster, offered me, namely, to add, by way of a postscript, a supplementary chapter outlining some of the ideas that during the last two decades have evolved in my theory of conscience. As to the wider field that this book concerns, i.e., the interrelationship between psychotherapy and theology, the reader will find pertinent discussions in my two most recent books published in English (and in English only), *Psychotherapy and Existentialism** and *The Will to Meaning*.† In each of these books one chapter explicitly deals with religious issues, and there are scattered references to this topic as well.

The updated bibliography at the end of this volume will enable the reader to locate further publications, not only those dealing with the relationship between religion and psychiatry but also publications covering the whole area of logotherapeutic teachings and practices.

However, the main thesis propounded in the lecture entitled "The Unconsious God" remains still valid and tenable. There is, in fact, a religious sense deeply rooted in each and every man's unconscious depths. In two of my

---

* Viktor E. Frankl, *Psychotherapy and Existentialism: Selected Papers on Logotherapy* (New York: Washington Square Press, 1967, and Touchstone paperback, 1968).

† Viktor E. Frankl, *The Will to Meaning: Foundations and Applications of Logotherapy* (New York and Cleveland: The World Publishing Company, 1969; paperback edition, New York: New American Library, 1970).

books, *Man's Search for Meaning** and the above-mentioned *The Will to Meaning*, evidence has been advanced to support my contention that this sense may break through unexpectedly even in cases of severe mental illness such as psychoses. For example, a student of mine at the United States International University, San Diego, California, wrote:

In the mental hospital, I was locked like an animal in a cage, no one came when I called begging to be taken to the bathroom, and I finally had to succumb to the inevitable. Blessedly, I was given daily shock treatment, insulin shock, and sufficient drugs so that I lost most of the next several weeks. . . .

But in the darkness I had acquired a sense of my own unique mission in the world. I knew then, as I know now, that I must have been preserved for some reason—however small, it is something that only I can do, and it is vitally important that I do it. And because in the darkest moment of my life, when I lay abandoned as an animal in a cage, when because of the forgetfulness induced by EST I *could not* call out to Him, He was there. In the solitary darkness of the "pit" where men had abandoned me, *He was there*. When I did not know His Name, He was there; God was there.

Likewise, such unexpected religious feelings may break through under other circumstances, as was the case with a man who wrote from prison:

I am at the age of 54 financially ruined, in jail. At the beginning of this incarceration (8 months ago) everything

* Viktor E. Frankl, *Man's Search for Meaning: An Introduction to Logotherapy* (Boston: Beacon Press, 1959; New York: Touchstone, Simon and Schuster, 1973).

looked hopeless and irrevocably lost in chaos that I could never hope to understand, much less to solve.

Endless months passed. Then, one day I had a visit by a court psychiatrist to whom I took an immense liking, right from the start, as he introduced himself with a very pleasant smile and a handshake, like I would be still "somebody," or at least a human being. Something deep and unexplainable happened to me from there on. I found myself reliving my life. That night, in the stillness of my small cell, I experienced a most unusual religious feeling which I never had before; I was able to pray, and with utmost sincerity, I accepted a Higher Will to which I have surrendered the pain and sorrow as meaningful and ultimate, not needing explanation. From here on I have undergone a tremendous recovery.

This happened in Baltimore County Prison in April of this year. Today, I am at complete peace with myself and the world. I have found the true meaning of my life, and time can only delay its fulfillment but not deter it. At fifty-four, I have decided to reconstruct my life and to finish my schooling. I am sure I can accomplish my goal. I have also found a new great source of unexpected vitality—I am able now to laugh over my own miseries, instead of wallowing in the pain of irrevocable failure, and somehow there are hardly any great tragedies left. . . .

But one may discuss religion irrespective of whether it is unconscious or conscious, for the question confronting us is more basic and radical. First, we must ask ourselves whether this is a legitimate area for psychiatric exploration. Lately, I have come to draw the line of demarcation between religion and psychiatry ever more sharply.* I have learned, and taught, that the difference

* Viktor E. Frankl, *The Doctor and the Soul: From Psychotherapy to Logotherapy.* (New York: Alfred A. Knopf, Inc.; second, expanded edition, 1965; paperback edition, New York: Vintage Books, 1973).

between them is no more nor less than a difference between various dimensions. From the very analogy with dimensions, however, it should become clear that these realms are by no means mutually exclusive. A higher dimension, by definition, is a more *inclusive* one. The lower dimension is included in the higher one; it is subsumed in it and encompassed by it. Thus biology is overarched by psychology, psychology by noölogy, and noölogy by theology.

The noölogical dimension may rightly be defined as the dimension of uniquely human phenomena. Among them, there is one which I regard as the most representative of the human reality. I have circumscribed this phenomenon in terms of "man's search for meaning." Now, if this is correct, one may also be justified in defining religion as man's search for *ultimate* meaning. It was Albert Einstein who once contended that to be religious is to have found an answer to the question, What is the meaning of life? If we subscribe to this statement we may then define belief and faith as *trust* in ultimate meaning. Once we have conceived of religion in this way—that is, in the widest possible sense—there is no doubt that psychiatrists are entitled also to investigate this phenomenon, although only its human aspect is accessible to a psychological exploration.

The concept of religion in its widest possible sense, as it is here espoused, certainly goes far beyond the narrow concepts of God promulgated by many representatives of denominational and institutional religion. They often depict, not to say denigrate, God as a being who is primarily concerned with being believed in, by the greatest possible number of believers, and along the lines of a specific creed, at that. "Just believe," we are told, "and everything will be okay." But alas, not only is this order based on a distortion of any sound concept of deity, but even more important, it is doomed to failure: obviously, there are certain activities that simply cannot be commanded, demanded or ordered, and as it happens, the triad "faith, hope and love" belongs to this class of activities that elude an approach with, so to speak, "command characteristics." Faith, hope and love cannot be established by command simply because they cannot be established at will. I cannot "will" to believe, I cannot "will" to hope, I cannot "will" to love—and least of all can I "will" to will.

Upon closer investigation it turns out that what underlies the attempt to establish faith, hope, love and will by command is the manipulative approach. The attempt to bring these states about at will, however, is ultimately based on an inappropriate objectification and reification of these human phenomena: they are turned into mere things, into mere objects. However, since faith, hope, love and will are so-called "intentional" acts or activities, along the lines of the terminology coined by Edmund Husserl and Max Scheler, the founders of the school of "phenomenology," these activities are directed to "intentional" referents—in other words, to objects of their own. To the extent that one makes intentional acts into objects, he loses sight of *their* objects. Nowhere, to my knowledge, is this brought home to us more strikingly than with the uniquely human phenomenon laughter: you cannot order anyone to laugh—if you want him to laugh, you must tell him a joke.

But isn't it, in a way, the same with religion? If you want people to have faith and belief in God, you cannot rely on preaching along the lines of a particular church but must, in the first place, portray your God believably—

and you must act credibly yourself. In other words, you have to do the very opposite of what so often is done by the representatives of organized religion, when they build up an image of God as someone who is primarily interested in being believed in, and who rigorously insists that those who believe in him be affiliated with a particular church. Small wonder that such representatives of religion behave as though they saw the main task of their own denomination as that of overriding other denominations.

Certainly the trend is away from religion conceived in such a strictly denominational sense. Yet this is not to imply that, eventually, there will be a universal religion. On the contrary: if religion is to survive, it will have to be profoundly personalized.

This does not mean that there is no need for symbols and rituals. Even the die-hard agnostic and atheist cannot completely dismiss symbols. Consider the Russians who once constructed a monument to express symbolically their indebtedness and gratitude to the thousands of dogs that had been sacrificed by Pavlov in the course of his famous conditioned-reflex experiments—what a purely symbolic gesture, pointless by the utilitarian yardstick adopted by dialectical materialism, and yet extremely meaningful to the heart of the Russian nation. A heart like that of which Blaise Pascal once observed that it has reasons that are unknown to reason (*le coeur a ses raisons que la raison ne connaît point*). The heart of man defies even Marxist indoctrination.

To all appearances, religion is not dying, and insofar as this is true, God is not dead either, not even "after Auschwitz," to quote the title of a book. For either belief in God is unconditional or it is not belief at all. If it is unconditional it will stand and face the fact that six million died in the Nazi holocaust; if it is not unconditional it will fall away if only a single innocent child has to die—to resort to an argument once advanced by Dostoevski. There is no point in bargaining with God, say, by arguing: "Up to six thousand or even one million victims of the holocaust I maintain my belief in Thee; but from one million upward nothing can be done any longer, and I am sorry but I must renounce my belief in Thee."

The truth is that among those who actually went through the experience of Auschwitz, the number whose religious life was deepened—in spite, not to say because, of this experience—by far exceeds the number of those who gave up their belief. To paraphrase what La Rochefoucauld once remarked with regard to love, one might say that just as the small fire is extinguished by the storm whereas a large fire is enhanced by it—likewise a weak faith is weakened by predicaments and catastrophes whereas a strong faith is strengthened by them.

VIKTOR E. FRANKL

THE UNCONSCIOUS GOD

ECCE LABIA MEA NON COHIBUI

1
The Essence
of Existential Analysis

Arthur Schnitzler, Vienna's famous poet and contemporary of Sigmund Freud, has been quoted as saying that there are really only three virtues: objectivity, courage, sense of responsibility. It would be tempting to allot to each of these virtues one of the schools of psychotherapy that have emerged from the Viennese soil.

It is obvious that the virtue of courage fits Adlerian psychology. The Adlerian, after all, regards his entire therapeutic procedure, in the final analysis, as nothing but an attempt at encouraging the patient. The purpose of this encouragement is to help the patient overcome his inferiority feelings, which Adlerian psychology considers to be a decisive pathogenic factor.

In the same way, another of the virtues mentioned fits Freudian psychoanalysis—that of objectivity. What else could it have been that enabled Sigmund Freud, like Oedipus, to look into the eyes of the Sphinx—the human *psyche*—and to draw out its riddle at the risk of a most dreadful discovery? In his time such an undertaking was colossal, and so was his accomplishment. Up to then psychology, particularly so-called academic psychology, had shunned everything that Freud then made the focus of his teaching. As the anatomist Julius Tandler jokingly called the "somatology" which was taught in Vienna's junior high schools "anatomy with the exclusion of the genital," likewise Freud could have said that academic psychology was psychology with the exclusion of the libidinal.

However, psychoanalysis not only adopted objectivity —it succumbed to it. Objectivity eventually led to objectivation, or reification. That is, it made the human person into an object, the human being into a thing. Psychoanalysis regards the patient as ruled by "mechanisms," and it conceives of the therapist as the one who knows how to handle these mechanisms. He is the one who knows the technique by which disturbed mechanisms may be repaired.

But cynicism lurks behind an interpretation of psychotherapy in terms of mere technique. It is true that we can see the therapist as a mere technician only if we have viewed the patient in the first place as some sort of a machine. Only an *homme machine*, I would say, is in need of a *médecin technicien*.

How is it that psychoanalysis arrived at this technically minded, mechanistic view? This is understandable considering the intellectual climate in which psychoanalysis emerged, but it must also be understood in the context of the social milieu of the time—a milieu full of prudery. It was a response—a reaction, to be sure, which is "reactionary," in that today it is out of date in many respects. But Freud not only reacted to his time, he also acted out of his time. When he formed his teaching he did so completely under the impact and influence of Associationism, which was then beginning to dominate psychology. Associationism, however, was the product of naturalism, an ideology typical of the late nineteenth century. Within Freud's teaching it makes itself most conspicuous in two basic characteristics of psychoanalysis: its psychological atomism and its theory of psychic energy.

Psychoanalysis sees the whole that the human psyche is, atomistically insofar as it conceives of the psyche as being pieced together out of separate parts, i.e., various drives, which in turn are composed of so-called "drive components." Thus the psyche is not only atomized but an-atomized, and the analysis of the psyche is turned into its anatomy. In the same way, the wholeness of the human person is in some sense destroyed. One could even say that psychoanalysis depersonalizes man. On the other hand, it personifies the individual aspects within the totality of the psyche, aspects which are often in conflict with one another. Sometimes they are not only personified but even demonified, e.g., when the id or the superego is dealt with as if it were a relatively independent, pseudo-personal power in itself.

In this way psychoanalysis destroys the unified whole that the human person is, and then has the task of reconstructing the whole person out of the pieces. This is most noticeable in Freud's hypothesis that the ego is made up out of "ego drives." According to this hypothesis the censor, which represses the drives, is itself a drive. Just consider the following statement quoted from Freud's *Three Essays on the Theory of Sexuality*: ". . . the production of sexual excitation . . . produces a store of energy which is employed to a great extent for purposes other than sexual

—namely . . . (through repression . . .) in building up the subsequently developed barriers against sexuality"* To me this is comparable to claiming that a builder who has constructed a building out of bricks is himself built of bricks, for that which builds a barrier against sexuality cannot itself be made up by sexuality. What here comes to the fore is the materialism that permeates the psychoanalytic way of thinking. This materialism inherent in psychoanalysis is also what ultimately accounts for its atomism.

We have pointed out that in addition to atomism, psychoanalysis is just as well characterized by energism. Psychoanalysis, in fact, operates constantly with the concepts of instinctual energism and emotional dynamism. Drives as well as drive components work the same way as what is called in physics a "parallelogram of forces." But on what are these forces working? The answer is—the ego. The ego in the psychoanalytic view is ultimately a plaything of the drives. Or as Freud himself once said, the ego is not the master in its own house.

Psychological phenomena are therefore reduced to drives and instincts and thus seem to be totally determined by them—determined in the sense of cause and effect. Being human is *a priori* interpreted by psychoanalysis in terms of being driven. That is also the ultimate reason why the ego, once it has been dismembered, has to be reconstructed out of the drives.

With such an atomistic, energistic and mechanistic concept of man, psychoanalysis sees him in the final analysis as the automaton of a psychic apparatus. And that is

---

* Sigmund Freud, *Three Essays on the Theory of Sexuality* (London: Image, 1949).

precisely the point where existential analysis comes in. It sets another concept of man over against the psychoanalytic one. It is no longer focused on the automaton of a psychic apparatus but rather on the autonomy of spiritual existence. "Spiritual" is being used here without any religious connotation, of course, but rather just to indicate that we are dealing with a specifically human phenomenon (in contrast to the subhuman phenomena that we share with other animals). In other words, the "spiritual" is what is human in man.

And thus we come back to Schnitzler's list of virtues. Just as we could apply the virtue of objectivity to psychoanalysis and that of courage to Adlerian psychology, so it is apt to apply to existential analysis the virtue of responsibility. In fact, existential analysis interprets human existence, and indeed being human, ultimately in terms of being responsible. At the time we introduced the term "existential analysis"* in 1938, contemporary philosophy offered the word "existence" to denote that specific mode of being which is basically characterized by being responsible.

If we were to give a quick account of what led existential analysis to recognize responsibleness as the essence of existence, then we would have to begin with an inversion of the question, What is the meaning of life? I made this inversion in my first book, *Ärztliche Seelsorge* (Vienna: Deuticke, 1946)† when I contended that man

---

* Cf. Viktor E. Frankl, *"Zur geistigen Problematik der Psychotherapie,"* Zentralblat für Psychotherapie, 10, 33 (1938).

Viktor E. Frankl, *"Philosophie und Psychotherapie. Zur Grundlegung einer Existenzanalyse,"* Schweizerische medizinische Wochenschrift, 69, 707 (1939).

† The English version is *The Doctor and the Soul: From Psychotherapy to Logotherapy* (New York: Alfred A. Knopf, Inc., 1965).

is not he who poses the question, What is the meaning of life? but he who is asked this question; for it is life itself that poses it to him. And man has to answer to life by answering for life; he has to respond by being responsible; in other words, the response is necessarily a response-in-action.

While we respond to life "in action" we are also responding in the "here and now." What is always involved in our response is the concreteness of a person and the concreteness of the situation in which he is involved. Thus our responsibility is always responsibility *ad personam* plus *ad situationem*.

Existential analysis, in the form of logotherapy, has a psychotherapeutic method to offer because it is concerned with the neurotic mode of being, in particular, and is intended to bring man, the neurotic in particular, to an awareness of his responsibleness. As we see, also in existential analysis man becomes conscious of something. But whereas in psychoanalysis it is the instinctual of which he becomes conscious, in existential analysis, or logotherapy, he becomes conscious of something spiritual, or existential. For it is only from the viewpoint of man's spirituality, or existentiality, that being human can be described in terms of being responsible. What comes to consciousness in existential analysis, then, is not drive or instinct, neither id drives nor ego drives, but self. Here it is not the ego that becomes conscious of the id but rather the self that becomes conscious of itself—it meets itself.

2

The Spiritual Unconscious

We now arrive at an essential revision of the prevalent concept of the unconscious, or more specifically, of its extent. We now have to revise its limits because it turns out that there is not only an instinctual unconscious but a spiritual unconscious as well. Thus the content of the unconscious has been expanded insofar as the unconscious itself has been differentiated into unconscious instinctuality and unconscious spirituality.

Previously we have tried to supplement psychotherapy in the strict sense of the word by introducing logotherapy as a psychotherapy centered and focusing on the spiritual—which constitutes the noölogical dimension as distinct from the psychological dimension. Having thus included the spiritual into psychology in general, we now include it in particular into depth psychology—that is, into the psychology of the unconscious.

Freud saw only unconscious instinctuality, as represented in what he called the id; to him the unconscious was first and foremost a reservoir of repressed instinctuality. However, the spiritual may also be unconscious; more-over, existence is *essentially* unconscious, because the foundation of existence is never and cannot be fully reflected upon and thus cannot be fully aware of itself.

Since the instinctual and the spiritual are both unconscious, and the spiritual may be conscious as well as unconscious, we now have to ask ourselves how sharp these two distinctions are. The border between conscious and unconscious is a very fluid one—it is permeable—for there is a constant transition from one to the other. We need only consider what psychoanalysis has termed repression: in the act of repression something conscious becomes unconscious; and vice versa, in the removal of repression something unconscious is made conscious again.

In contrast to the "fluid" border between conscious and unconscious, the line between the spiritual and the instinctual cannot be drawn sharply enough. This fact has been expressed most concisely by Ludwig Binswanger when he spoke of "instincts and spirit" as "incommensurable concepts." Since human existence is spiritual existence, we now see that the distinction between conscious and unconscious becomes unimportant compared with another distinction: the real criterion of authentically human existence only derives from discerning whether a given phenomenon is spiritual or instinctual—whereas it is relatively irrelevant whether it is conscious or unconscious. This is due to the fact that—in contrast to the psychoanalytic concept—being human is not being driven but "deciding what one is going to be," to quote Jaspers (*entscheidendes Sein*), or to quote Heidegger: *Dasein.* I would say that being human is being responsible—existentially responsible, responsible for one's own existence.

Existence thus may well be authentic even when it is

unconscious; on the other hand, man only exists authentically when he is not driven but, rather, responsible. Authentic existence is present where a self is deciding for himself, but not where an id is driving him.

It might be said that psychoanalysis has id-ified, and de-selv-ified, human existence. Insofar as Freud degraded the self to a mere epiphenomenon, he betrayed the self and delivered it to the id; at the same time, he denigrated the unconscious, in that he saw in it only the instinctual and overlooked the spiritual.

Before, we stated that the line between the spiritual —as the human in man—and the instinctual cannot be drawn sharply enough. In fact we may conceive of it as an ontological *hiatus* which separates the two fundamentally distinct regions within the total structure of the human being. On one side is existence, and on the other side is whatever belongs to facticity: whereas existence, according to our definition, is in essence spiritual, facticity contains somatic and psychic "facts," the physiological as well as the psychological. And whereas the line between existence and facticity, that ontological *hiatus*, must be drawn as sharply as possible, within the realm of facticity the line between the somatic and the psychic cannot be drawn clearly. Any physician who has ever tried to elucidate the multidimensional etiology of a psychosomatic condition knows very well how difficult it is to differentiate between psychogenic and somatogenic components.

As the dichotomy "conscious–unconscious" has become only a secondary issue, so the age-old psychophysical problem now proves to have lost its primary significance. It has to recede behind the much more essential problem of spiritual existence versus psychophysical facticity. This issue is not only a problem of greater ontological import, but also one of greater psychotherapeutic relevancy. After all, a psychotherapist is continually concerned with spiritual existence in terms of freedom and responsibility, and with marshaling it against the psychophysical facticity which the patient is prone to accept as his fate. The awareness of freedom and responsibleness which constitutes authentic humanness must be set against this neurotic fatalism.

But we must not neglect the fact that being human is always individualized being. As such, it is always centered around a core, and this core is the person, who, in the words of Max Scheler, is not only the agent but also the "center" of spiritual activity. I would say that this spiritual personal center is encompassed by the peripheral psychophysical layers. Now instead of talking of spiritual existence and psychophysical facticity, we may speak of the spiritual person and "its" psychophysical overlay. By "its" we mean to emphasize that the person "has" a psychophysical overlay, whereas the person "is" spiritual. After all, I am not really justified in saying "my self," not even "myself," since I do not "have" a self, but I "am" a self. If anything, I can "have" an id, but precisely in the sense of psychophysical facticity.

Being centered around the existential, personal, spiritual core, human being is not only individualized but also integrated. Thus the spiritual core, and only the spiritual core, warrants and constitutes oneness and wholeness in man. Wholeness in this context means the integration of somatic, psychic and spiritual aspects. It is not possible to stress enough that it is only this threefold wholeness which makes man complete. In no way are we justified in speaking of man in terms of only a "somatic-psychic whole." Body and psyche may form a unity

—a psychophysical unity—but this unity does not yet represent the wholeness of man. Without the spiritual as its essential ground, this wholeness cannot exist. As long as we speak only of body and psyche, wholeness has not yet come in.

As far as the structure of the human being is concerned, we have so far given preference to the model of layers versus the model of strata. In fact, we have replaced the vertical hierarchy of unconscious, preconscious and conscious strata by the model of concentric layers, a model propounded by Max Scheler.

But why not go one step further by combining the strata model with the layers model? Why not conceive of the concentric layers as the ground plan of a three-dimensional structure? We would only have to imagine that the personal core—the spiritual center that is encompassed by the peripheral somatic and psychic layers—is prolonged so that we would have to conceive of it as an axis. This axis then would extend, together with the peripheral layers encompassing it, throughout the unconscious, preconscious and conscious strata.

In other words, we have put together two two-dimensional models and made them into a three-dimensional one. Now the two former models have been reconciled, as it were, having become the two-dimensional projections of a three-dimensional model that more accurately depicts the human reality we are describing. Any human phenomenon, whether belonging to the personal axis or to the somatic-psychic layers, may occur on any level, the unconscious, preconscious or conscious.

To take up once more the issue of "depth psychology" we have to extend the meaning of this concept, because up to now depth psychology has followed man into the depth of his instincts, but too little into the depth of his spirit. Since "depth" refers to the unconscious, it necessarily follows that the person in his depth, the spirit in its depth, or for that matter, human existence in its depth is essentially unconscious. This is due to the fact that spiritual activity so absorbs the person as the executor of spiritual acts that he is not even capable of reflecting on what he basically is. The self does not yield to total self-reflection.* In this sense, human existence is basically unreflectable, and so is the self in itself. Human existence exists in action rather than reflection.

Insofar as human existence cannot fully be reflected upon by itself, it cannot be fully analyzed either. That is why existential analysis can never be an analysis of existence but can only be an analysis toward existence. Human existence remains an *Urphänomen*, i.e., an unana-

---

* Cf. Friedrich von Schiller's epigram, "*Spricht die Seele, so spricht, ach, schon die Seele nicht mehr,*" which means, "As soon as the soul starts talking, it is no longer the soul who is talking." Likewise, we might say that once the self reflects on itself, it is no longer the true self that exhibits itself.

lyzable, irreducible phenomenon. And this holds for each of its basic aspects, e.g., such human phenomena as consciousness and responsibleness. If these are to be illuminated, we have to transcend the ontic plane toward the ontological dimension. Within the plane of psychological immanance, both consciousness and responsibleness are and remain unsolvable problems. However, as soon as we transpose them into the ontological dimension they cease to be problems. For then they are taken as *Urphänomene*, constitutive of human existence, or in Heideggerian terms, they are "existentials," attributes that belong to the very foundations of human existence.

To sum up, spiritual phenomena may be unconscious or conscious; the spiritual basis of human existence, however, is ultimately unconscious. Thus the center of the human person in his very depth is unconscious. In its origin, the human spirit is unconscious spirit.

This is not unlike the eye—precisely at the place of its origin the retina has its "blind spot," as the entrance of the optical nerve is called in anatomy. Likewise, the spirit is "blind" precisely where it has its origin—precisely there no self-observation, no mirroring of itself is possible; where the spirit is "original" spirit, where it is fully itself, precisely there it is also unconscious of itself. We may therefore fully subscribe to what has been said in the Indian Vedas: "That which does the seeing, cannot be seen; that which does the hearing, cannot be heard; and that which does the thinking, cannot be thought."

However, the spirit is not only unconscious where it originates, that is, in its depth, but also in its height as well. In fact, that which has to decide whether something is to be conscious or unconscious is itself unconscious. Just consider the fact that there is something in the sleeping man that decides whether or not he should continue sleeping. This guard, for example, has the sleeping mother awake as soon as the breathing of her child becomes irregular, whereas she sleeps through loud noises from the street. Even in states of hypnosis this guard does not fail —even here the subject wakes up as soon as something he does not want is about to happen. Only in deeper states of narcosis is this guard put to silence—put to sleep itself. Otherwise it keeps watch over man as if it were conscious, and yet it is at best quasi-conscious. True, it somehow must know what happens around the sleeper; but this has nothing to do with actual consciousness. That which decides whether an experience will become conscious or will remain unconscious is itself unconscious. In order to make such a decision, however, it must somehow be able to discern. Since both deciding and discerning are spiritual acts, again it follows that these spiritual acts not only can be but must be unconscious—unconscious in the sense of being unreflectable.

3
Existential Analysis
of Conscience

The phenomenon of conscience serves well as a model to illuminate further our concept of the spiritual unconscious. As we said in the preceding chapter, conscience, along with responsibleness, is a true *Urphänomen*, an irreducible phenomenon that is inherent in the human being as a deciding being, as *entscheidendes Sein*. Now whatever we have previously attempted to derive theoretically must let itself be shown phenomenologically through the medium of the phenomenon of conscience. In fact, conscience reaches down into unconscious depths, stems from an unconscious ground; and it is precisely those momentous, authentic—existentially authentic—decisions that take place completely unreflectedly and thus unconsciously. Precisely where it originates, conscience delves down into the unconscious.

In this sense conscience is irrational; it is alogical or, better put, prelogical. Just as there is a prescientific understanding and, ontologically even prior to it, a prelogical understanding of being, so there is likewise a premoral understanding of meaning, and this is conscience. The premoral understanding of meaning precedes any understanding of values, and therefore is not contingent upon morals.

In which sense may we regard conscience as being irrational? At least while in action it never can be explained in rational terms; such explanation is possible only "after the fact." Moral self-scrutiny also is possible only afterward. The judgments of conscience, in the final analysis, are inscrutable.

If we ask ourselves why conscience necessarily operates in an irrational way, then we have to consider the following. What is disclosed to consciousness is something that *is*; however, what is revealed to conscience is not anything that is but, rather, something that *ought to be*. What merely ought to be is not real, but is something to make real; it is no actuality but mere possibility (although in a higher, in the ethical sense, such a possibility again represents a necessity). Insofar as that which has been disclosed to conscience is still to be actualized, the question emerges how it could be realized unless it were somehow anticipated in the first place. Such anticipation, however, can only be enacted through intuition.

So conscience is essentially intuitive. To anticipate what is not yet, but is to be made real, conscience must be based on intuition. And it is in this sense that conscience may be called irrational. But is not conscience in this respect analogous to love? Is not love just as irrational, just as intuitive? In fact, love does intuit, for it also envisions something that is not yet real. What love anticipates, however, is not an ethical necessity but, rather, a personal possibility. Love reveals potentialities dormant in the loved person, which he still has to make real.

However, concern with mere possibilities rather than actualities is not the only common denominator of love and conscience. It is one reason why both must operate on an intuitive level; a second reason is to be seen in the fact that both love and conscience have to do with something, or someone, absolutely unique.

It is the task of conscience to disclose to man the *unum necesse*, the one thing that is required. This one thing, however, is absolutely unique inasmuch as it is the unique possibility a concrete person has to actualize in a specific situation. What matters is the *unique* "ought to be" which cannot be comprehended by any universal law. No generally valid law in the sense of Immanuel Kant's "categorical imperative" can get hold of it, but only an "individual law" in the sense of Georg Simmel. And above all, it can never be comprehended in rational terms, but only intuitively.

Insofar as conscience intuitively discloses such concrete, individual possibilities of meaning, one might be tempted to think of the way conscience operates as instinctive, and thus to speak of conscience itself as an ethical instinct. But once we take a closer look we see that this ethical instinct markedly deviates from what generally is called instinct, i.e., the biological instinct. The instinct of the animal has an overall aim—is directed toward something general and also operates "in general." It operates in the "innate releasing schemes," or "mechanisms," according to Konrad Lorenz. The instinctive reactions of animals to certain environmental signs and signals (*Merkmale* and *Wirkmale* according to von Uexküll) are strictly schematic and rigid in that they are fixed for each species. The effectiveness of such schemes thus depends on the fact that they only work for the species in general, for the benefit of the greatest number, whereas in individual cases they not only fail but sometimes even mislead the animal to act "unwisely." The same instinctive pattern of reaction that preserves and saves, for example, the majority of ants may in a given case mean the destruction of a particular ant: the "wisdom" of the instincts requires that such a "sacrifice" be made for the sake of the whole ant colony. The vital instincts in principle neglect the individual.

The "ethical instinct" is entirely different. In contrast to vital instincts, the effectiveness of the ethical instinct depends on the fact that its target is not anything general but something individual, something concrete. And just as the animal is at times misled by the vital instincts, so may man go astray, ironically, by obeying the precepts of moral reason which, as such, only deal with generalities, whereas the ethical instinct alone enables him to discover the unique requirement of a unique situation, the *unum necesse*. Only conscience is capable of adjusting the "eternal," generally agreed-upon moral law to the specific situation a concrete person is engaged in. Living one's conscience always means living on a highly personalized level, aware of the full concreteness of each situation. Indeed, conscience has comprehended the concrete "whereness" (*Da*) of my personal being (*Sein*) all along.

Love also parallels conscience with respect to the uniqueness of its target. Just as conscience aims at the uniqueness of possibilities dormant in each life situation, so love aims at the equally unique potentialities dormant in a loved person. Even more, love alone enables the loving person to grasp the uniqueness of the loved person. In this sense love has a significant cognitive function, and certainly this was appreciated by the ancient Hebrews when they used the same word for the act of love and the act of knowledge.

Are we also justified to compare the quality of deciding and choosing in love and in conscience? Does love even have to do with decision and choice? Certainly it does. To be sure, the choice of a partner is only a true choice when it is not dictated by drives. As long as, for example, an unconscious image, an "imago," determines my "choice," it cannot be a matter of love. And as long as a self is driven by an id to a Thou, it is not a matter of love, either. In love the self is not driven by the id, but rather the self chooses the Thou.

However, not only love and moral conscience are rooted in the emotional and intuitive, nonrational depths of the spiritual unconscious, but also what I would call the artistic conscience. Thus, ethics and aesthetics as well have their foundation and basis within the spiritual unconscious. In fact, in his creative work the artist is dependent on sources and resources deriving from the spiritual unconscious.* The nonrational intuition of conscience is paralleled by the inspiration of the artist. Artistic creation emerges out of recesses in a realm that can never be fully illuminated. We clinicians observe time and again that excessive reflection on the creative process proves to be harmful. Forced self-observation may become a severe handicap to the creativity of the artist. An attempt to produce on a conscious level what must grow in unconscious depths, the attempt to manipulate the primal creative process by reflecting on it, is doomed to failure. Reflection comes in only later.

* Viktor E. Frankl, *Psychotherapy and Existentialism: Selected Papers on Logotherapy* (New York: Washington Square Press, 1967; Touchstone paperback, 1968).

We know a case in which a violinist always tried to play as consciously as possible. From putting his violin in place on his shoulder to the most trifling technical detail, he wanted to do everything consciously, to perform in full self-reflection. This led to a complete artistic breakdown. Therapy had to start with eliminating this tendency to overbearing self-reflection and self-observation, or, in the terminology of logotherapy, "hyper-reflection." Therapy had to be aimed at what we call in logotherapy "de-reflection." Treatment had to give back to the patient his trust in the unconscious, by having him realize how much more musical his unconscious was than his conscious. As a matter of fact, this treatment oriented toward the patient's reliance on his unconscious brought about the release of the artistic "creative powers" of his unconscious. De-reflection liberated the creative process from the inhibiting effects of any unnecessary reflection.

This brings to the fore the question, What should be the goal of psychotherapy? No longer is one allowed to believe that the goal of psychotherapy consists in making something conscious at any price. Becoming conscious is no more than a transitory stage in the psychotherapeutic process. It has to make conscious the unconscious—including the spiritual unconscious—only in order to allow it finally to recede back to unconsciousness. To put it in the terms of the Scholastics, what therapy has to achieve is to convert an unconscious *potentia* into a conscious *actus*, but to do so for no other reason than to restore it eventually as an unconscious *habitus*. It is the task of the therapist, in the final analysis, to reinstate the spontaneity and naïveté of an unreflected existential act.

This might seem to imply that artistic creativity, or any spiritual activity, is just a matter of emotions and feelings. But the concept of emotion and feeling has today become too vague, and it is important to bear in mind Scheler's distinction between feeling as a mere "emotional state" (*Gefühlszustand*) and feeling as an "intentional feeling" (*intentionales Gefühl*), i.e., a feeling directed to an intentional referent. As a matter of fact, such intentional feelings may well have their roots in the spiritual unconscious, but the mere emotional states have as little to do with spiritual existence as do any states caused by instinctual drives.

To say that the concept of feeling is vague in no way implies that feeling itself is vague. At least as far as "intentional feeling" is concerned, rather the contrary: feeling can be much more sensitive than reason can ever be sensible.

The difficulties we run into when we try to explore the necessarily unconscious sources of spiritual activity are demonstrated by the fact, trivial as it might seem, that people have always made jokes and have laughed but there is still no full scientific explication of phenomena such as joking and laughing. This shows just how independent an act can be from any reflective understanding of it.

In conclusion, where the spiritual self steeps itself in its unconscious depths, there occur the phenomena of conscience, love and art. Where it happens the other way around, however—that is to say, where the somatopsychic id intrudes into consciousness—there we have to deal with a neurosis or a psychosis, depending on whether the case is psychogenic or somatogenic.

4

Existential Analysis of Dreams

From what has been discussed it seems to follow that the spiritual unconscious would be extremely difficult to illuminate. And yet there is a way by which the unconscious—including its spiritual aspect—yields itself to exploration, namely, by way of dreams. Since Freud introduced the classical method of dream interpretation, based on free associations, we have learned to avail ourselves of this opportunity. This is also done in existential analysis, although our goal is to lift not only instinctual but also spiritual phenomena into consciousness—and into responsibleness. After all, dreams are the true creations of the unconscious, and therefore we may expect that not only elements of the instinctual unconscious will come to the fore, but elements of the spiritual unconscious as well. Thus we use the same method Freud did when he tracked down the instinctual unconscious, but we may use the method to a different end, the disclosure of the spiritual unconscious.

Conscience has proved to be an apt model to demonstrate how the spiritual unconscious operates. The same model now may well serve us in the context of dream analysis. To take an example:

A woman dreamed that, along with her dirty wash, she took a dirty cat to the laundry. When she came to pick up the laundry she found the cat dead. She came up with the following free associations: As to "cat," she said that she loved cats above all; but equally she loved her daughter—her only child—"above all." From this we may infer that "cat" stands for "child." But why is the cat "dirty"? That became clear as soon as we learned from the patient that recently she had been worrying about the gossip surrounding her daughter's love life—her "dirty linen," too, was being washed in public. That was the reason why the patient, as she admitted, was constantly watching and hounding her daughter. The dream therefore expressed a warning to the patient not to torment her daughter with exaggerated demands of moral "cleanliness" or she might lose her child.

We cannot see any reason why we should give up such a straightforward interpretation, open to whatever presents itself in the dream, in deference to the preconceived idea that behind it infantile-sexual contents *must* be hidden. The phenomena of the spiritual unconscious are empirical facts, and confronted with them, we wish to embrace the great virtue of psychoanalysis: objectivity. Such objectivity, however, should not only be demanded of the analysand but of the analyst as well. Just as unconditional honesty is required of the analysand, likewise the analyst should be equally honest and not close his eyes to the facts of the spiritual unconscious.

Consider the dream of another patient:

The patient reports a dream that kept recurring frequently, even within one night. He would dream that he was in another city and wanted to phone a certain lady. But the dial was so gigantic—it contained some hundred numbers—that he never succeeded in placing the call. After waking, the patient realized that the number he meant to dial was not the lady's but that of a record company for which he was then working with great financial success. As a matter of fact, the patient was a composer of popular music. Now, in the discussion of his dream it turned out that he had actually spent a very satisfying time in the city he dreamed of, composing religious music, whereas his work, although outwardly successful, did not give him inner fulfillment. Except for his composing, he cherished no pleasant memories connected with that city. In particular, he had no longing for that lady, with whom he had never had any erotic relationship. On the other hand, he spontaneously declared that the gigantic dial signified the trouble he had when choosing. (To understand the symbolism of the dream we have to realize that in German the same word, *wählen*, is used for choosing and dialing.) What then was the patient's choice? It did not refer to a number to dial but rather the vocation to choose—specifically, to the choice between keeping a well-paying, unsatisfying job as a composer of hits and becoming a writer of religious music. Suddenly the essential meaning of the dream became clear. Although in vain, the patient had been struggling to be "connected" again, to be "re-connected." Now we have just to replace *re-conexio* by *religio*, which in Latin means the same, and it is obvious that the dream expressed the patient's desire to find his way back to his true religious and artistic vocation.

This dream, unlike the previous one, does not present a warning to the dreamer but rather expresses a self-reproach. In both cases, however, the dream is an utter-ance of conscience—in the second case, not only of ethi-cal conscience but also of the artistic conscience; but both dreams are expressions of the spiritual unconscious. In the second case, it was a religious problem that consti-tuted the latent dream content. In the following, the same problem is encountered on a more manifest level:

A patient dreamed his father handed over some saccharine to him, but he refused it with the proud re-mark that he would rather drink coffee or tea bitter than sweetened with some sort of sugar substitute. The free association went literally as follows: "handed over—tra-dition; but the tradition I got from my father is our re-ligion." The patient continued to associate, saying that the evening before the dream he had read a magazine article recording a dialogue between an existential phi-losopher and a theologian. The argument of the existential philosopher seemed very plausible to him, and above all he was impressed by the philosopher's rejection of ex-istentially inauthentic religiosity, in particular where the philosopher refused "to flee into a realm of belief and dream," and then exclaimed, "What sort of a motive is it to want to be happy? What we want is truth." So also here, in his wide-awake life, the patient renounced in-authenticity. The same evening the patient had heard a radio sermon which he felt somehow to be cheap consola-tion—and somehow "sweetish." It also turned out that at one point in the magazine article the question was asked, "What is it like when the taste [!] for living is lost?" With that in mind, we can understand quite well why the ex-istentially inauthentic religious tradition was associated with the realm of taste, and why the image chosen in the dream was the sugar substitute saccharine, taking the place of the genuine sweetener. This choice of symbols became fully clear when we learned that the patient's good-luck piece was a religious icon, and that he disguised it from unwanted viewers by carrying it in a small wooden box which originally had served as a package for saccharine.

In other dreams expressive of the spiritual unconscious we meet the patient's personal problems pertaining not only to religion in general, but also to religious institutions in particular:

A woman dreamed she went to the Alser Church. To that she associated: "On the way to my psychiatrist I pass the Alser Church, and when I pass it I often think, I am on the way to God—not through the church directly, but through psychotherapy. My way to God goes, so to speak, through the doctor. On my way back from the therapy session, of course, I again pass the Alser Church, and so going to therapy is only a detour to the church. The dream itself continues as follows: "The church seems to be deserted." Interpretation: That the church is deserted signifies that the patient has deserted the church. In fact, she had turned her back on the church. The dream continues: "The church is entirely bombed out; the roof has fallen in, and only the altar remains intact." Interpretation: The inner shock the patient experienced from the war has shaken her spiritually, but has also opened her eyes to the central place, the altar, of religion in life. "The blue heavens shine through here; the air is free." Interpretation: Those inner shocks have freed her eyes to see the celestial. "But above me is still the remainder of the roof, beams that threaten to fall down, and I am afraid of that." Interpretation: The patient is afraid of falling back and of once more being buried in debris.

"And I flee into the open, somewhat disappointed." Interpretation: The patient actually had recently gone through disappointments not only with her own affirmation of religion, but also with religious institutions. Complete affirmation of her religion had been hampered by occasional impressions of pettiness and narrowness on the part of some priests and theologians.

It was not surprising that the patient had troubles with institutionalized religion for she said she had experienced ecstatic mystical states several times. Therefore it was interesting to explore this side of her religious problematic, and to see how far this aspect of the patient's spiritual unconscious found expression in her dreams:

"I find myself on St. Stephen's Square." (This is the center of Catholic Vienna.) "I stand in front of the main door of St. Stephen's Cathedral, and I see that it is closed." Interpretation: She has no access to Christianity. "In the Cathedral it is dark, but I know God is there." To this the patient produces as a spontaneous association the following quotation from the Psalms: "Truly, you are a hidden God." The dream continued: "I am searching for the entrance." Interpretation: She is searching for an entrance to Christianity. "It is almost twelve noon." Interpretation: It is high time. "Father N. N. is preaching inside." (Father N. N. was for this patient somehow representative of Christianity.) "Through a small window I can see his head." Interpretation: What he represents goes beyond the small part she sees of him. "I want to get inside." Interpretation: She wants to turn away from his appearance and turn toward the essence. "I am running through narrow passages." The connection between narrowness (*Enge*) and anxiety (*Angst*) is well known; the patient, indeed, is anxiously and impatiently striving to reach her goal. "I have a box of candy with me, with the inscription on it, 'God calls.' " Interpretation: She is called to a religious life, which is the goal toward which she is so impatiently striving, and the way to this goal already contains the sweetness of ecstatic mystical experiences. "I take a candy out of the box and eat it, although I know that it may make me sick." The patient had repeatedly reported that she deliberately exposed herself to the risk of insanity as a potential result of her mystic states, i.e., the risk that they might make her "sick." "I am afraid someone may see the inscription on the candy box; I am ashamed and start to erase the inscription." The patient knew that her "case" was going to be published and so tried everything she could to thwart its publication.

Here we are confronted with a fact that will come to be quite important, namely, that people are sometimes ashamed of their religiousness and try to conceal it. The mistake is often made of confounding such shame with neurotic inhibition. Shame, however, is a perfectly natural attitude. Since Max Scheler's work on this subject, we know that shame has a distinctive protective function in love. Its task is to prevent something from becoming a mere object—an object for onlookers. So we could say the cause of love is served by not being observed. Love flees publicness, for man is afraid that what is sacred to him might be profaned by becoming public. More specifically, this profanation might occur through a loss of immediacy in giving oneself to, and loving, the other. Such immediacy, however, is threatened not only by becoming an object for others, but by becoming an object for one's own self-observation as well. In both cases the immediate, original genuineness of love is liable to vanish; its existentiality is liable to dwindle into mere facticity. Being is turned into being observed, be it by oneself, be it by others. Loving is in danger of being "de-selv-ified" and "id-ified."

Now, something analogous may happen to religiousness. The quality of intimacy so characteristic of love is no less characteristic of religion. It is intimate in two senses: it is *intimum* in the sense of innermost, and second, it is, like love, protected by shame. Genuine religiousness, for the sake of its own genuineness, hides from the public. That is why religious patients often do not want to deliver their intimate experiences into the hands of people who would perhaps lack understanding and thus misinterpret them. Such patients may be afraid that a psychiatrist will try to "unmask" their religiousness as "nothing but" the manifestation of unconscious psychodynamics, of conflicts or complexes. Or they may fear just as much that their religiousness will be interpreted as something impersonal—be it in the sense of unconscious "archetypes" or of the "collective unconscious."

One can understand why the patient shied away from seeing herself one day published as a "case," and her religious feelings thereby somehow debased into the mere object of a detached scientific investigation. Of course, patients are reluctant not only to become "cases" in publications, but also to be "demonstrated" before a public—such as being part of clinical demonstrations of psychotherapy to medical students. In the classroom setting we could witness time and again that patients who are quite ready to talk about their sexual lives in the most intimate and even perverse details are the same ones who display marked inhibitions as soon as the discussion turns to their intimate religious life.

For example, during one of these demonstrations a

patient happened to be asked if she could reproduce a dream, and she came up with the following one: "I am in the middle of a great crowd of people; it is like a fair. Everyone is moving in one direction, while I myself try to go in the opposite direction." Interpretation: In the "fair" that this world is, the great masses of people are all alike. The patient, however, is swimming against the current. "Somehow I know the direction in which I have to go, for from the heavens shines a light which I am going toward. This light gets brighter and brighter and finally condenses into a figure." Interpretation: At first the patient knew the direction only approximately, but now she knows it more precisely. Then we asked what sort of a figure it was. With that, however, the patient became embarrassed, and after much hesitation she asked with an imploring look, "Do I really have to talk about that?" Only after much persuasion did she let out her secret and murmur, "The figure was Christ." In her dream her conscience had demanded that she follow Christ.

In this dream there is scarcely any religious problem left, since to this patient it was unquestionable that she had to take the religious path. In contrast, the dreams reported before this one showed clear-cut religious problems, be they manifest or latent, depending on whether the religiousness was conscious to the patient or had been repressed by him into the unconscious. That repression of religiousness can occur is no longer a surprise when we realize the intimate quality inherent in genuine religiousness. Nor is it surprising occasionally to find flagrantly religious motifs in dreams of people who are manifestly irreligious, because we have seen that there is not only repressed and unconscious *libido,* but also repressed and unconscious *religio.*

One of my patients once spontaneously declared: "How come I am ashamed of whatever is religious, that it seems to me bothersome and ridiculous? Well, I know very well myself why I feel so ashamed about my religious longings: underlying all the psychotherapeutic treatment I have had these last twenty-seven years was the more or less tacit conviction on the part of my doctors that such longings are nothing but unrealistic, baseless speculation. As they put it, only the tangible is real, and everything else is nonsense, caused by a trauma or by the wish to escape life by fleeing into disease. So whenever I expressed my longing for God I was almost afraid they would bring in the straitjacket. Until now every type of psychotherapy missed the point."

A patient of mine wanted to discover why she had such a dislike for Christianity. She had not practiced her religion since childhood. In a deliberate combination of logotherapy and suggestive measures I gave her the posthypnotic suggestion, "Tonight I shall receive the answer from my dreams." This is the dream that she reported the next day:

"I am in the town where I spent my childhood. I am waiting for a train to Vienna." The patient thereby sums up her way from the past into the present. "Dr. X lives there. I want to visit him." Dr. X is a well-known psychotherapist and a good friend of the patient's family. Thus the dream indicates a need for psychotherapy. "I don't know what Dr. X's address is. I ask a woman and she says, 'Near the church.'" The patient knows that her recovery in psychotherapy can only be completed through religion. "I am thinking in the dream, Eventually I shall find the church again." So she is optimistic. Needless to say, the "church" here means more than just the building.

Thus the dream indicates her hope and conviction that she will find her way back to religion. "But everything is different from what it used to be." To find this way back is not so simple for an adult who has been chased through the hell of life and of doubt. "I wonder which street to take." Which way should she take to come back to religion? "I have been walking a long time. I feel doubtful." In the dream this doubt refers to the way to Dr. X, but in reality it is doubt about God. "A little girl is standing in front of me and gives me information." Spontaneously the patient observed that this girl represented herself as she was in her childhood. So I asked her whether she knew the biblical saying, "You must become like children again," and the patient told me that this passage had always impressed her deeply. And what was the information this girl handed out in the dream? "Near the church; but you have taken the wrong way—you must go back." So the patient feels that first she must go back to the simplicity of children as this characterizes their faith. "I am thirsty." To this the patient associates a verse from the Psalms: "As the hart panteth after the water brooks, so panteth my soul after thee. . . ." The dream continues: "The child draws clear water from a spring, and now I am actually going back." The way back means psychotherapy—more specifically, existential analysis. "Suddenly I see poplars lying across the street." These fallen poplars signify the difficulties and relapses that had emerged during therapy. "But then the way is clear again, and in the distance is the church—a miraculous cathedral, milky white, like the one in Caen." In her own attempt to interpret the dream it came out that, when driving to France on a trip some years before, she had looked forward to seeing the cathedral because she had known it from pictures and admired it very much. But when her party arrived in Caen it was so dark and so foggy that she never actually saw the cathedral. We feel justified in interpreting the transformation of the cathedral, which she had never seen but had so much longed for, into the splendorous sight of the church in the dream, as a symbol of the transformation of the patient's concept of God that had taken place through treatment—namely, the transition from the *Deus absconditus* into the *Deus revelatus*.

5

The Transcendent Quality
of Conscience

In the existential analysis of dreams in the preceding chapter, the psychological fact of repressed and unconscious religiousness became obvious. And the empirical results of existential analysis come up to its ontological
expectations. In fact, if the existential analysis of conscience is carried further, one will be confronted with a
very significant finding, which may best be described as
the transcendent quality of conscience. To illuminate this
finding, start with the following assumptions:

All freedom has a "from what" and a "to what." The
"from what" of man's freedom is his being driven; and the
"to what" is his being responsible, his having conscience.
These two facets of the human condition are best expressed by a simple admonition from Maria von Ebner-
Eschenbach: "Be the master of your will and the servant
of your conscience!" From this sentence, from this moral
imperative, we would like to start to illuminate what we
have called the transcendent quality of conscience.

"Be the master of your will. . . ." Well, I am already

the master of my will insofar as I am human and fully aware of my humanness—that is to say, insofar as I am interpreting this humanness in terms of responsibleness. But if I am also to be "the servant of my conscience," then I may ask whether this conscience has not to be something other than I myself; might it not be something higher than he who merely perceives its "voice?" In other words, I cannot be the servant of my conscience unless I understand conscience as a phenomenon transcendent of man. So I cannot consider conscience simply in terms of its psychological facticity, but must also grasp it in its transcendent essence. I can be the servant of my conscience only when the dialogue with my conscience is a genuine *dia-logos* rather than a mere *mono-logos*. This, however, can only be so when my conscience transcends my self, when it is the mediator of something other than my self.

It would seem, therefore, that the phrase "the voice of conscience," common to so many languages, is based on a mistake. If conscience "had" a voice it could not "be" a voice itself—the voice of transcendence. Then man would only overhear this voice—it would not stem from him. But only the transcendent quality of conscience makes it possible to understand man in depth, or more specifically, to understand his being a person. The very term "person," seen in this light, takes on a new meaning, for now one may say: Through the conscience of the human person, a trans-human agent *per-sonat*—which literally means, "is sounding through." It is not up to us to answer the question of what this "agent" is, since our concern with the origin of conscience is anthropological rather than theological. Nonetheless we may be justified in claiming that this trans-human agent must necessarily be of a personal nature. More correctly, however, we would have to speak of a transpersonal agent of which the human person is but the "image."

So conscience is not only a fact within psychological immanence but also a referent to transcendence; only with reference to transcendence, only as some sort of transcendent phenomenon, can it really be understood. It is like the human navel, which would appear meaningless if it were taken as an isolated phenomenon; the navel can only be understood in the context of the prenatal history, for it points beyond the individual to his origin in his mother. It is the same with conscience; it can only be fully understood as a phenomenon pointing to its own transcendent origin. As long as we consider man as an isolated being without the context of his origin, some things about him must elude our understanding; and what holds for the ontogenesis of man also is true of ontology. We cannot ontologically understand such a human phenomenon as conscience unless we reach back to its transcendent origin. Conscience is fully understandable only against the background of a trans-human dimension. To explain man's being free, the existential quality of the human reality would do; however, to explain his being responsible, the transcendent quality of conscience must be considered.

So conscience, which we have taken as our model of the spiritual unconscious, is seen to have a key position in disclosing to us the essential transcendence of the spiritual unconscious. The psychological fact of conscience is but the immanent aspect of a transcendent phenomenon; it is only that piece of the whole phenomenon which seeps into psychological immanence.

If conscience is the voice of transcendence it is thus

itself transcendent. Viewed in this light, an irreligious man is one who does not recognize this transcendent quality. Needless to say, the irreligious man also "has" a conscience, and he also is responsible; he simply asks no further—neither what he is responsible to, nor from what his conscience stems. But this is no reason for the religious man to become haughty. Consider the biblical story of Samuel: When Samuel was a boy he once spent a night in the temple with the high priest Eli. He was awakened by a voice calling him by name. He rose and asked Eli what he wanted; but the high priest had not called him and told him to go back to sleep. The same thing happened a second time, and only when it happened a third time did the high priest tell the boy that the next time he heard his name called, he should stand up and say, "Speak, Lord; for thy servant heareth."

If Samuel failed to recognize that the call came to him from transcendence, how much more difficult it must be for an ordinary person to discern the transcendent character of the voice he perceives through his conscience. And why should we be surprised if he takes this voice for something that is rooted merely within himself?

The irreligious man thus proves to be the one who takes his conscience in its psychological facticity. Facing it as merely an immanent fact, he stops—stops prematurely—for he considers conscience the ultimate "to what" he is responsible. However, conscience is not the last "to what" of responsibleness, but the next to last. On his way to find the ultimate meaning of life, the irreligious man, as it were, has not yet reached the highest peak, but rather has stopped at the next to highest. (This, of course, is the way the *religious* man looks at the irreligious.) And what is the reason the irreligious man does not go further?

It is because he does not want to lose the "firm ground under his feet." The true summit is barred from his vision; it is hidden in the fog, and he does not risk venturing into it, into this uncertainty. Only the religious man hazards it.

The more religious a man is, the more he will respect the decision of his fellow man not to go further. After all, it is precisely the religious man who should respect the freedom of such a choice, because he is the one who believes man to be created free. And this freedom includes the possibility of saying no, for instance, by deliberately refusing to accept any religious *Weltanschauung*. To be sure, among those who have committed themselves to an atheistic or agnostic world view, there are some who are ready to accept the concept of transcendence, but do not feel that this necessitates that they speak of "God." However, there are others who do not see any reason why not to denote transcendence by the age-old word "God."

Conscience not only refers to transcendence; it also originates in transcendence. This fact accounts for its irreducible quality. Therefore, if we raise the question of the origin of conscience, there can be no psychological answer but only an ontological one. Any attempt at a mere ontic reduction, any attempt to reduce conscience to psychodynamics, proves futile. This was clearly seen by the nineteenth-century writer Hebbel when he wrote in a letter of May 13, 1857, addressed to Uechtritz: "Conscience stands in striking contrast to any values that might be put forward by materialism. If one tries to reduce conscience to the sexual drive or to the instinct of propagation—something that surely will happen sooner or later, if it has not already happened—even then conscience will be neither explained away nor done away with." What Hebbel prophesied here has in the meantime happened. Indeed, psychoanalysis has tried to explain conscience in psychodynamic terms, reducing it to the superego, and deducing the superego from the introjected father image.

However, just as the self cannot be identified with the ego, likewise conscience cannot be identified with the superego. Rather one must acknowledge the irreducibility of these two phenomena: the existential quality of the self and the transcendent quality of conscience. As to the first phenomenon, man's being responsible can never be traced back to his being driven—the self can never be traced back to any drives or instincts. The self has the function of repressing and sublimating the drives and instincts but can itself never be derived from them. Even if instinctual energy is utilized in repression and sublimation, that which puts this energy into motion cannot itself be explained merely in terms of instinctual energy. Or has anyone seen a river building its own power plant? It was man who dammed the water to utilize its energy.

But just as drives and instincts cannot repress themselves, likewise the self cannot be responsible merely to itself. The self cannot be its own lawgiver. It can never issue any autonomous "categorical imperative," for a categorical imperative can receive its credentials only from transcendence. Its categorical character stands and falls with its transcendent quality. It is true that man is responsible for himself, but ultimately he is not responsible before himself. Not only man's being free, but also his being responsible requires an intentional referent. Just as freedom means little, indeed means nothing, without a "to what," likewise responsibleness is incomplete without a "to what."

Goethe once said: *"Alles Wollen ist ja nur ein Wol-*

len, weil wir eben sollten"—whenever man wills, this act of will always presupposes a grasp of what he ought to do. The "ought" is ontologically prior to the will. Just as I can only answer if I am first questioned, just as each reply requires a "to what," and such a "to what" must be prior to the reply itself, so the "to what" of all responsibleness must necessarily be prior to responsibleness itself.

What I feel that I ought to do, or ought to be, could never be effective if it were nothing but an invention of mine—rather than a discovery. Jean-Paul Sartre believes that man can choose and design himself by creating his own standards. However, to ascribe to the self such a creative power seems to be still within the old idealistic tradition. Is it not even comparable to the fakir trick? The fakir claims to throw a rope into the air, into the empty space, and claims a boy will climb up the rope. It is not different with Sartre when he tries to make us believe that man "projects" himself—throws himself forward and upward—into nothingness.

It may be said that the psychoanalytic superego theory comes down to the contention that the ego pulls itself by the bootstraps of the superego out of the bog of the id. However, the superego is not the only thing regarded as an (introjected) father image; the God concept too is interpreted in terms of a (projected) father image. Now let us for heuristic purposes play off the psychoanalytic view against the theological. A Copernican switch would be the result. For theology God is not a father image, but rather the father is an image of God. In this view the father is not the model of divinity, but on the contrary, God is the model of paternity. Biographically and biologically the father is first; theologically, however, God is first. Psychologically the relationship between the child and his father is prior to the relationship between man and God; theologically, however, my natural father, and in this sense my creator, is but the first representative of a supernatural father and creator of the universe.

Many psychoanalysts have interpreted all religion merely in terms of sublimation and thus have reduced all religious experience, be it conscious or unconscious and repressed, to infantile sexuality. To this one might say: No one will be able to make us believe that man is a sublimated animal once we can show that within him there is a repressed angel.

6

Unconscious Religiousness

By examining the results attained in the preceding five chapters together with results previously obtained by existential analysis, it can be seen that the approach has been developed in three main stages:

The starting point* was the basic phenomenological fact that being human is being conscious and being responsible, culminating in a synthesis of both—namely, in one's consciousness of his responsibleness.

The second stage of development was reached when existential analysis ventured into unconscious spirituality. In 1926 logotherapy—the clinical application of our existential analytic approach—had extended the scope of psychotherapy beyond the *psyche*, beyond the psychological dimension to include the noological dimension, or the *logos*; in the second stage, the *unconscious*

---

* Viktor E. Frankl, *The Doctor and the Soul: From Psychotherapy to Logotherapy* (New York: Alfred A. Knopf, Inc.; second, expanded edition, 1965; paperback edition, New York: Vintage Books, 1973). The original (German) version was published in 1946.

logos was disclosed with the discovery of a spiritual unconscious in addition to the instinctual unconscious. In these unconscious spiritual depths the great existential choices are made. It follows, then, that man's being responsible reaches down into an unconscious ground; thus, besides conscious responsibleness there must also be unconscious responsibleness.

With the discovery of the spiritual unconscious, existential analysis eluded the peril to which psychoanalysis had succumbed, namely, of id-ifying the unconscious. With the concept of the spiritual unconscious, existential analytic logotherapy also avoided any one-sided intellectualism and rationalism in its theory of man. Logos is deeper than logic. Thus the fact that man can no longer be considered as a totally rational being has been recognized by logotherapy without falling prey to the *other* extreme, i.e., idolizing the irrational and the instinctual, as did psychoanalysis.

Now, in its third stage of development, existential analysis has uncovered—within the spiritual unconscious —unconscious religiousness. This unconscious religiousness, revealed by our phenomenological analysis, is to be understood as a latent relation to transcendence inherent in man. If one prefers, he might conceive of this relation in terms of a relationship between the immanent self and a transcendent thou. However one wishes to formulate it, we are confronted with what I should like to term "the transcendent unconscious"—as part and parcel of the spiritual unconscious. This concept means no more or less than that man has always stood in an intentional relation to transcendence, even if only on an unconscious level. If one calls the intentional referent of such an unconscious relation "God," it is apt to speak of an "unconscious God." This, however, in no way implies that God is unconscious to himself, but rather that God may be unconscious to man and that man's relation to God may be unconscious.

In the Psalms mention is made of "the hidden God," and Hellenistic culture dedicated an altar to "the unknown God." Similarly, our concept of an unconscious God refers to man's hidden relation to a God who himself is hidden.

The phrase "unconscious God" could be misinterpreted in three main ways. First of all, it could be misunderstood as pantheistic. It would be a complete misconception to assume that the unconscious is itself divine. It is only related to the divine. That man has an unconscious relation to God does not at all mean that God is "within us," that he "inhabits" our unconscious—all this is but a notion of theological dilettantism.

Another potential misinterpretation of the unconscious God concept would be to take it in the sense of occultism. The paradox of an "unconscious knowledge" of God would be mistakenly interpreted to mean that the unconscious is omniscient, or even knows better than the conscious self. Not only is the unconscious not divine, but furthermore, it does not possess any attribute of the divine, and thus lacks divine omniscience as well. As the first misinterpretation had to be rejected as theological dilettantism, the second one amounts to instant metaphysics.

No knowledge can come to know itself, to judge itself, without rising above itself. In the same vein, no science can weigh its own results and realize their implications without transcending its own ontic sphere and subjecting itself to ontological scrutiny. That is the reason which compelled us to go beyond the borders of strict science in order to see how the result of our phenomenological, and in this sense empirical, investigation matched up with the ontological expectations. This makes it even more important to keep the firm ground of empirical and clinical data under our feet lest we fall into what we denoted as theological dilettantism and instant metaphysics. Our task is to start with simple experiential facts and to evaluate them along the lines of traditional psychiatric methodology—for example, by invoking the classical method of free association in our dream analyses. To be sure, while so doing we paid due tribute to phenomenological "facts" as well. These facts, too, are "factual," and they are so to the extent that they do not allow for any further analytical reduction. Consider the flagrantly religious dreams of what were known to be manifestly irreligious patients. What is most striking in such dreams is an ecstatic experience of bliss that was unknown to the patient in his waking life. It is simply impossible to insist that behind such an experience there must be a sexual meaning—unless we choose to violate our intellectual honesty by pressing phenomena into the Procrustean bed—not to say, the Procrustean couch—of preconceived patterns of interpretation.

And now to the third and most important potential misinterpretation: it cannot be emphasized strongly enough that not only is the unconscious neither divine nor omniscient, but above all man's unconscious relation to God is profoundly personal. The "unconscious God" must not be mistaken as an impersonal force operant in man. This misunderstanding was the great mistake C. G. Jung fell prey to. Jung must be credited with having discovered distinctly religious elements within the unconscious. Yet he misplaced this unconscious religiousness of man, failing to locate the unconscious God in the personal and existential region. Instead, he allotted it to the region of drives and instincts, where unconscious religiousness no longer remained a matter of choice and decision. According to Jung, something within me is religious, but it is not I who then is religious; something within me drives me to God, but it is not I who makes the choice and takes the responsibility.

For Jung, unconscious religiousness was bound up with religious archetypes belonging to the collective unconscious. For him, unconscious religiousness has scarcely anything to do with a personal decision, but becomes an essentially impersonal, collective, "typical" (i.e., arche-typical) process occurring in man. However, it is our contention that religiousness could emerge least of all from a collective unconscious, precisely because religion involves the most personal decisions man makes, even if only on an unconscious level. But there is no possibility of leaving such decisions to some processes merely taking place in me.

For Jung and the Jungians unconscious religiousness has always remained something more or less instinctual. H. Bänziger, in a paper published in 1947 in the *Schweizerische Zeitschrift für Psychologie*, even bluntly declares: "We may speak of a *religious drive* just as we speak of sexual and aggressive drives" (the italics are Bänziger's!). But what sort of religion would that be—a religion to which I am driven, driven just as I am driven to sex? As for myself, I would not give a damn for a religiousness that I owed to some "religious drive." Genuine religiousness has not the character of driven-ness but rather that of deciding-ness. Indeed, religiousness stands with its deciding-ness—and falls with its driven-ness. In a word, religiousness is either existential or not at all.

For Jung, however—and in this respect he does not really differ from Freud—the unconscious, including its religious aspects, is something that determines the person. In contrast, we contend that the religious unconscious, or for that matter the spiritual unconscious, is a deciding being unconscious rather than a being driven by the unconscious. As we see it, the spiritual unconscious and, even more, its religious aspects, that is to say, what we have called the transcendent unconscious, is an existential agent rather than an instinctual factor. As such it belongs to spiritual existence rather than psychophysical facticity. This, however, was completely neglected by Jung when he wrote that archetypes should be understood as "a structural property or condition characteristic of the psyche which is in some way connected with the brain."* Thereby religiousness becomes entirely a matter of the somatic and psychic conditions of human existence—while it is really a matter of the spiritual person who builds on those conditions.

As Jung saw it, the religious archetypes are impersonal forms of the collective unconscious which can be unearthed as more or less preformed psychological facts, and as such pertain to psychophysical facticity. From this region they operate as autonomous powers—autonomous in the sense that they are independent of personal decisions. Our point of view, however, is that unconscious religiousness stems from the personal center of the individual man rather than an impersonal pool of images shared by mankind.

* Quoted from *Psychologie und Religion*, our translation.

If we respect the spiritual and existential character of unconscious religiousness—rather than allotting it to the realm of psychological facticity—it also becomes impossible to regard it as something innate. Since it is not tied up with heredity in the biological sense, it cannot be inherited either. This is not to deny that all religiousness always proceeds within certain preestablished paths and patterns of development. These, however, are not innate, inherited archetypes but pre-given cultural molds into which personal religiousness is poured. These molds are not transmitted in a biological way, but are passed down through the world of traditional symbols indigenous to a given culture. This world of symbols is not inborn in us, but we are born into it.

Thus there are religious forms, and they wait to be assimilated by man in an existential way, i.e., to be made his own. But what serves this purpose is not any archetype, but rather the prayers* of our fathers, the rites of our churches and synagogues,† the revelations of our prophets and the examples set by saints and zaddiks. Culture offers enough traditional molds for man to fill with lived religion—no one has to invent God. On the other

---

* In my book *The Will to Meaning* I have expressed my conviction that there is a dimensional barrier between the human world and the divine world, a barrier that prevents man from really speaking of God. He "cannot speak of God but he may speak to God. He may pray," I have said in this context. It is noteworthy, however, that a full awareness of this insurmountable inadequacy of the God concept can, as it were, be built in in a prayer, forming part of its contents. For an example, I may refer to the Hebrew prayer for the dead, Kaddish, more specifically, a passage to the effect that God is "high above all the blessings and hymns, praises and consolations which are uttered in the world."

† Much of what is derogatively called "organized religion" rather deserves the name "organic religion" because it has grown organically instead of being fabricated and propagated as ideologies are.

hand, no one carries Him along in the form of an innate archetype.

Primary religiousness therefore must not simply be identified with primitive or archaic religiousness. On the other hand, it is true time and again that primary religiousness which has fallen prey to repression comes to the surface in the form of a naïve or childlike faith. But nothing else should be expected, for such religiousness necessarily is associated with experiential material accrued during childhood. In fact, whenever an existential analysis unearths this material and releases it from repression, we are confronted with a faith that indeed is childlike in the truest, best sense of the word. No matter how childlike and naïve it may be, it is in no way primitive, nor is it archaic in the sense of Jung's archetypes. If one embarks on an unbiased analysis, he will not be confronted with elements of a pseudo-archaic mythology, but rather with religious experiences engraved in memories from one's childhood.

Existential analysis has moved even further beyond Freud's view of religion. It is no longer necessary to ponder "the future of an illusion," but our thoughts do revolve around the apparent timelessness of a reality—around the ever-presence of that reality which man's intrinsic religiousness has revealed itself to be. It is a reality in the strict sense of phenomenological empiricism. To be sure, it also is a reality that can remain, or again become, unconscious, or be repressed. Precisely in such cases, however, it is the task of logotherapy to re-mind the patient of his unconscious religiousness—that is to say, to let it enter his conscious mind again. After all, it is the business of existential analytic logotherapy to trace the neurotic mode of being to its ultimate ground. Some-

times the ground of neurotic existence is to be seen in a
deficiency, in that a person's relation to transcendence is
repressed. But although concealed in "the transcendent
unconscious," repressed transcendence shows up and
makes itself noticeable as an "unrest of the heart." In my
book *The Doctor and the Soul* I described a case in
which this restlessness precipitated a "psychosomatic,"
or really noo-somatic, heart condition. So what holds for
the unconscious in general is also true of unconscious
religiousness in particular: repression winds up in neurosis.

There is clinical evidence for this assertion. Take
the example of a patient suffering from a severe obsessive-compulsive neurosis that for decades had defied
long-term treatment by various psychoanalysts. The
symptomatological picture was dominated by the obsessive fear that whatever he did might eventuate in the
eternal damnation of his late mother or sister. For this
reason the patient would not accept a government position, for he would have had to take an oath of office,
which at some later time he might have violated, if only
in a trifling way. In consequence, mother and sister
would be damned. The patient had also evaded marriage, simply because he would have had to say "I do" at
the wedding, and if he were ever somehow to go against
his marriage vows that could also have led to the damnation of his dead mother and sister. He had not bought a
radio just because, in the moment he was going to buy it,
the obsessive thought went through his head that if he
did not immediately grasp a certain technical detail his
mother and sister would have to face a terrible fate in
hell.

Confronted with such an abundance of more or less

religious references in the patient's account, we asked him what his attitude was toward religion. To our surprise, it turned out that he considered himself a full-fledged "freethinker." More specifically, he declared himself to be a follower of Haeckel (a popularizer of a biologically oriented materialism well known around the turn of the century). And with obvious pride he related how much his understanding of modern physics had advanced through private studies; the theory of the electron, for example, he had completely mastered. To the question whether he knew anything about religious matters, he indeed admitted that he knew the prayer book but only "as the criminal knows the code of law." By this he meant that he was aware of it but did not care for it. To the question whether, then, he was irreligious, he responded, "Who can say that of himself? Sure, I am irreligious intellectually, but emotionally I still might believe. Intellectually I believe only in natural laws—not in anything such as a God who rewards and punishes." And behold, the same individual who uttered these words had shortly before, when reporting on his sexual impotence, remarked, "At that moment I was haunted by the obsessive idea that God could take revenge on me."

Freud, in *The Future of an Illusion*, said, "Religion is the universal compulsive neurosis of mankind; like that of the child, it derives from the Oedipal complex, from the relationship to the father." In view of the case history abstracted above, we are tempted to reverse Freud's statement and dare to say compulsive neurosis may well be diseased religiousness. In fact, clinical evidence suggests that atrophy of the religious sense in man results in a distortion of his religious concepts. Or, to put it in a less clinical vein, once the angel in us is repressed, he turns into a demon. There is even a parallel on the socio-cultural level, for time and again we watch and witness how repressed religion degenerates into superstition. In our century, a deified reason and a megalomanic technology are the repressive structures to which the religious feeling is sacrificed. This fact explains much of the present condition of man, which indeed resembles a "universal compulsive neurosis of mankind," to quote Freud. Much of man's present condition? Yes—with one exception: religion.

With special reference to technology, however, one is reminded of a dictum by Goethe: "He who possesses art and science also has religion." But today we know only too well where man would wind up if he had science and nothing beyond it: soon the only thing that would be left of all his science would be the atom bombs he possessed.

But let us turn away from problems of humanity and return to the compulsive neurosis of the individual. In concluding this chapter we might venture to say God is a "vengeful God" indeed, for neurotic existence in some cases seems to be the toll that a crippled relation to transcendence takes on man.

7
Psychotherapy and Theology

In conclusion of this book we may well ask what bearing all the questions raised might have on research and practice in the field of psychiatry. After all, it is not for the medical profession to be interested in theological problems. When such matters come into discussion, the physician is bound to unconditional tolerance. Least of all is a physician who personally is religious released from this obligation. He will only be interested in a spontaneous breakthrough of religiousness on the part of the patient. And he will be patient enough to wait for such a spontaneous development to take place. This should not be difficult for him since precisely he, as a religious person, is convinced that even in a manifestly irreligious person there must be latent religiousness. After all, the religious psychiatrist believes not only in God, but also in an unconscious belief on the part of the patient. In other words, he believes that his own God is "the unconscious God" of the patient. And, at the same time, he believes that this unconscious God is one who has simply *not yet* become conscious to the patient.

We have said that religion is genuine only where it is existential, where man is not somehow driven to it, but commits himself to it by freely choosing to be religious. Now we have seen that the existentiality of religiousness has to be matched by its spontaneity. Genuine religiousness must unfold in its own time. Never can anyone be forced to it. So we may say, to genuine religiousness man cannot be driven by an instinct—nor pushed by a psychiatrist.

As Freud has taught us, the process by which unconscious material becomes conscious has a therapeutic effect only if the process takes place spontaneously. The working through of repressed material is based on its spontaneously breaking through, and I think that something analogous also holds for repressed religiousness. Here, to exert any pressure along the lines of a preestablished program would be self-defeating; in this case, intention would thwart the effect. This is a fact of which even the clergy is quite aware. Even the clergy would insist on the full spontaneity of true religiousness; all the more should a psychiatrist. I well remember, for example, how a priest described being called to the deathbed of a man whom he knew to be irreligious. The man had simply felt the need to speak out his mind before he died, and had for this purpose chosen the priest. The priest told me that he had refrained from offering the last rites to the man for the simple reason that he had not spontaneously asked for them. So great was the priest's own insistence on spontaneity!

But should we psychiatrists be more priestly than the priests? Should we not instead have at least as much respect as this priest had for the free decisions of our patients, particularly in religious matters?

But time and again psychotherapists try even to outdo the priests. This is just hubris. The function of the psychiatrist cannot be distinguished sharply enough from the mission of the clergy. Just as the irreligious psychiatrist should let the religious patient have his belief, likewise the religious psychiatrist must let the priest keep his priestly office.

Elsewhere we have shown that it is characteristic of obsessive-compulsive patients to be dominated by a Faustian will that everything be "one hundred percent," that absolute certainty be reached in their acts of cognition and decision. As it were, they are hung up on the promise of the serpent: *Eritis sicut Deus, scientem bonum et malum* (You will be like God, knowing what is good and what is evil). And of those psychotherapists who try to usurp the duties of the clergy, we may say that they wish *esse sicut pastores, demonstrantes bonum et malum*—they wish to be, not like God, but like the priests, not knowing, but showing what is good and what is evil.

We have often said that logotherapy is not meant to substitute for psychotherapy but, rather, to supplement it. Likewise we have often pointed out that what we call medical ministry is in no way supposed to replace the pastoral ministry. This, however, does not do away with the possibility that the psychiatrist, if need be, may take over the function of the priest. The following is an instance of how this can happen:

An old woman came to the psychotherapeutic outpatient clinic of our department to consult us on her severe depression. She had no family left since her daughter, her only child, had recently committed suicide. She could not get over that. After her mourning showed itself to be not pathological but a normal reaction, the psychiatrist cautiously asked her how she felt about religion. Since the patient said she was religious, he inquired why, then, she had not instead sought the help of a priest. She replied that she had gone to her priest, but he had not had even a few minutes for her. However, the psychiatrist, himself a religious man, could easily give this woman the consolation she needed—that consolation on the grounds of their common faith which her priest had not been able to provide. The situation required that the psychiatrist take the place of the priest in order to give religious comfort. This was not only his human right, but even his religious duty, for in this case one religious person was confronting another. What we wish to stress, however, is that the psychiatrist is never entitled to such a religious approach *qua* psychiatrist, but only as a religious person. Furthermore, only a psychiatrist who is himself a religious person is justified in bringing religion into psychotherapy. An irreligious psychiatrist never has the right to manipulate the patient's religious feelings by employing religion as just another useful tool to try—along with such things as pills, shots and shocks. This would be to debase religion and degrade it to a mere device for improving mental health.

Although religion might have a very positive psychotherapeutic effect on the patient, its intention is in no way a psychotherapeutic one. Although religion might secondarily promote such things as mental health and inner equilibrium, its aim does not primarily concern psychological solutions but, rather, spiritual salvation. Religion is not an insurance policy for a tranquil life, for maximum freedom from conflicts, or for any other hygienic goal. Religion provides man with more than psychotherapy ever could—but it also demands more of him. Any fusion of the respective goals of religion and psychotherapy must result in con-fusion. The fact remains that the intentions of the two are different— even if their effects might overlap. In the same vein, any attempt to merge the medical ministry with the pastoral one is to be rejected. There are some authors who propose that psychotherapy relinquish its autonomy as a science and its independence from religion in favor of seeing its function as that of an *ancilla theologiae*. As is well known, for centuries philosophy was allotted the role of such an *ancilla theologiae*, i.e., a handmaid in the service of theology.

However, just as the dignity of man is based on his freedom—to the extent that he may even say no to God —likewise, the dignity of a science is based on that unconditional freedom which guarantees its independent search for truth. And just as human freedom must include the freedom to say no, so the freedom of scientific investigation must face the risk that its results will turn out to contradict religious beliefs and convictions. Only a scientist who is ready to fight militantly for such an autonomy of thought may triumphantly live to see how the results of his research eventually fit, without contradictions, in the truths of his belief.

Speaking of dignity—be it the dignity of man or that of science—we may define it as the value of something *in itself*, as opposed to its value *for me*. Thus we could say that whoever tries to make psychotherapy into an *ancilla theologiae*, a servant to theology, not only robs it of the dignity of an autonomous science but also takes away the potential value it might have for religion. Because psychotherapy can be useful to religion only in terms of a by-product, or a side effect, and never if its usefulness is intended from the start. If psychotherapy is ever to serve religion—either by the results of its empirical investigation or by the therapeutic effects of treatment—psychotherapy has to refrain from setting any preconceived goals along religious lines. Only those results which have been obtained by independent research, uninfluenced by presuppositions borrowed from religion, can ever be of use and value for theology. And if psychotherapy is ever to offer evidence that the human psyche really is what we think it is, namely, *anima naturaliter religiosa* (religious by nature), such evidence can only be offered by a psychotherapy that is *scientia naturaliter irreligiosa*—that is to say, a psychotherapy that by its very nature is not and never can be religiously oriented.

The less psychotherapy condescends to serve theology as a handmaid, the greater will be the service it actually performs.

One need not be a servant to be able to serve.

Postscript 1975
New Research in Logotherapy

In the Preface to the American edition, I promised to examine some of those tenets which, since the first publication of *The Unconscious God* in German in 1947, have been further elaborated. Understandably, I will have to concentrate on conscience as one of the most important phenomena central to these tenets. According to the logotherapeutic theory, conscience has a very specific function. However, in order to make this function fully understood, I must first chart the motivation theory as it underlies logotherapy.

According to most of the current motivation theories, man is a being basically concerned with gratifying needs and satisfying drives and instincts; he does so, in the final analysis, only in order to alleviate the inner tension created by them, to the end of maintaining, or restoring, an inner equilibrium which is called "homeostasis." This is a concept originally borrowed from biology but which was eventually found even there to be no longer tenable. Ludwig von Bertalanffy had long maintained and demonstrated that primordial biological phenomena such as growth and reproduction cannot be explained along the lines of the homeostasis principle. Kurt Goldstein even proved that only a brain that is functioning pathologically is characterized by the attempt to avoid tension unconditionally. I for one think that man is never primarily concerned with any inner condition, such as the inner equilibrium, but rather with something or someone out there in the world, be it a cause to serve or a partner to love—and if he really loves the partner, he certainly does not just use him as a more or less apt means to the end of satisfying his own needs.

Thus, human existence—at least as long as it has not been neurotically distorted—is always directed to something, or someone, other than itself—be it a meaning to fulfill or another human being to encounter lovingly. I have termed this constitutive characteristic of human existence "self-transcendence."* What is called "self-actualization" is ultimately an effect, the unintentional by-product, of self-transcendence. So it turns out that Pindar's imperative that one should become what he is— in other words, that man should actualize his potentialities—is valid only if we add what Karl Jaspers once said: "What one is, he has become through that cause which he has made his own." Or, as Abraham H. Maslow put it, the "business of self-actualization" can best be carried out "via a commitment to an important job."†

Just as self-actualization can be obtained only

* Viktor E. Frankl, "Beyond Self-Actualization and Self-Expression," *Journal of Existential Psychiatry*, Vol. 1, No. 1 (Spring 1960), pp. 5–20.
† Abraham H. Maslow, *Eupsychian Management* (Homewood, Ill.: Irwin, 1965).

through a detour, through the fulfillment of meaning, so identity is available only through responsibility, through being responsible for the fulfillment of meaning. It is fitting that research conducted at Boston University, based on a new test that "measures the collective neurosis as formulated by logotherapy," shows that there "appears to be a negative correlation between the collective neurosis and responsibility."*

Therefore man is originally characterized by his "search for meaning" rather than his "search for himself." The more one forgets oneself—giving oneself to a cause or another person—the more *human* he is. And the more one is immersed and absorbed in something or someone other than oneself the more he really becomes *himself*. Just consider a child who, absorbed in play, forgets himself—this is the moment to take a snapshot; when you wait until he notices that you are taking a picture, his face congeals and freezes, showing his unnatural self-consciousness rather than his natural graciousness. Why do most people have that stereotyped expression on their faces whenever they are photographed? This expression stems from their concern with the impression they are going to leave on the onlooker. It is "cheese" that makes them so ugly. Forgetting themselves plus forgetting the present photographer plus forgetting the future onlooker would make them beautiful.

Forgetting themselves—and overlooking themselves. Consider the eye. The eye, too, is self-transcendent in a way. The moment it perceives something of itself, its function—to perceive the surrounding world visually—

* From personal communication received from Professor Orlo Strunk, Jr.

has deteriorated. If it is afflicted with a cataract, it may "perceive" its own cataract as what looks like a cloud; and if it is suffering from glaucoma, it might "see" its own glaucoma as a rainbow halo around the lights. Normally, however, the eye doesn't see anything of itself. Equally, by virtue of the self-transcendent quality of the human reality, the humanness of man is most tangible when he forgets himself—and overlooks himself!

One of the two aspects of self-transcendence, namely, reaching out for a meaning to fulfill, is identical with what I have come to call "the will to meaning." This concept, which occupies such a central place in the motivation theory of logotherapy, denotes the fundamental fact that normally—or in neurotic cases, originally—man is striving to find, and fulfill, meaning and purpose in life. This concept of a will to meaning has been empirically corroborated and validated by several authors, who based their research on tests and statistics. James C. Crumbaugh and Leonard T. Maholick devised their Purpose-in-Life Test,* and Elisabeth S. Lukas developed her Logo-Test. These tests were applied to thousands of subjects, and after the data had been computerized it was evident that the will to meaning is more than just the wishful thinking of some idealists.

Research conducted by S. Kratochvil and I. Planova of the Department of Psychology of the University of Brno, Czechoslovakia, offered evidence that "the will to meaning is really a specific need not reducible to other needs, and is in greater or smaller degree present in all human beings. The relevance of the frustration of this

* Psychometric Affiliates, P.O. Box 3167, Munster, Indiana, 46321.

need," the authors continue, "was documented also by case material, concerning neurotic and depressive patients. In some cases the frustration of the will to meaning had a relevant role as an etiological factor in the origin of the neurosis or of the suicidal attempt." Abraham H. Maslow goes further; to him the will to meaning is more than "an irreducible need"—he sees it as "man's primary concern."*

If there were still a need to demonstrate that the concept of a will to meaning has a realistic basis and is perfectly down to earth, one might consider the result of a survey published by the American Council on Education: among the 171,509 students screened, the highest goal— held by 68.1 percent—was "developing a meaningful philosophy of life."† There is also another statistical survey, conducted by Johns Hopkins University and sponsored by the National Institute of Mental Health: among 7,948 students at forty-eight colleges, only 16 percent said their first goal was "making a lot of money." Seventy-eight percent of the students, however, checked "finding a purpose and meaning to my life."‡

The findings collected by Johns Hopkins University are paralleled by those gathered by the University of Michigan: 1,533 working people were asked to rank various aspects of work in order of importance, and "good pay" came in a distant fifth. Small wonder that Joseph

---

* "Comments on Dr. Frankl's Paper," in Anthony J. Sutich and Miles A. Vich, eds., *Readings in Humanistic Psychology* (New York: The Free Press, 1969).
† Robert L. Jacobson, *The Chronicle of Higher Education* (Washington, D.C.: American Council on Education, January 10, 1972).
‡ *Los Angeles Times*, February 12, 1971.

Katz of the State University of New York, reviewing some recent opinion polls, said that "the next wave of personnel entering industry will be interested in careers with meaning, not money."*

As we see, the will to meaning "cannot be explained away as merely philosophical apparel for traditional dynamic concepts," to quote from a study by James C. Crumbaugh.† In fact, "current psychodynamic theory and the therapy based on it are too narrow in scope to explain the behavior of the younger generation and reach

---

* Joseph Katz, in *Psychology Today*, Vol. 5, No. 1 (June 1971). Seventy-eight percent . . . which, as it happens, is exactly the percentage of Polish youngsters who regarded it as their highest purpose in life "to improve their living standard" (*Kurier*, August 8, 1973). Apparently, Maslow's hierarchy of needs is applicable to the issue at hand: first one has to improve one's living standard, and only after this has been accomplished may he approach the task of "finding a purpose and meaning in his life." However, I regard this as a mistake. It goes without saying that someone who is ill wishes, in the first place, to become healthy. So, health will seem to constitute his supreme goal in life. But in actual fact, it is no more than a means to an end, because health is a precondition for attaining whatever might be considered the real meaning in a given instance. In other words, in such a case it is first mandatory to inquire what is the end that stands behind the means. And an appropriate method for such an inquiry may well be some sort of a Socratic dialogue. As we see, Maslow's motivation theory does not suffice here, for what is needed is not so much the distinction between higher and lower needs but, rather, an answer to the question of whether the individual goals are mere means or meanings.

In everyday life we are fully aware of this difference. If we did not recognize it, we wouldn't laugh at a comic strip that shows Snoopy complaining of his suffering from a feeling of meaninglessness and emptiness—until Charlie Brown comes in with a bowl full of dog food, and Snoopy exclaims, "Ah! Meaning!!" What makes us laugh is precisely the confusion of means and meaning: while food is certainly a necessary condition for survival, it is no sufficient condition to endow one's life with meaning and thus relieve the sense of meaninglessness and emptiness.

† "The Validation of Logotherapy," in R. M. Jurjevich, ed., *Direct Psychotherapy* (Coral Gables, Fla.: University of Miami Press, 1973).

them," as Z. J. Lipowski says.* What is even more important is the danger that man—and here again, particularly the younger generation—may be corrupted by being underrated. Conversely, if I am cognizant of the higher aspirations of man—such as his will to meaning—I am also able to muster and mobilize them.

I am always reminded, in this context, of the business my flight instructor calls crabbing. If there is a crosswind, say, from the north and the airport where I wish to land lies east and I fly east, I will miss my point of destination because my plane will drift to the southeast; so, in order to compensate for this drift, I have to fly my plane in a direction north of my point of destination, and this is called "crabbing." But isn't it the same with man? Doesn't he too wind up at some point that is lower than his destination unless he is seen on a higher level that includes his higher aspirations? What did my flight instructor say? If I fly east in a so-called crosswind condition, I will land south of east; if I head north of east, I will land east. Well, if I take man as he is, I make him worse; if I take him as he ought to be, I make him become what he can be. But this is no longer something my flight instructor told me, but, rather, a literal quotation from Goethe. . . .

If the concept of a will to meaning is idealistic at all, I would call such idealism the real realism. If we are to bring out the human potential at its best, we must first believe in its existence and presence. Otherwise man too will "drift"; he will deteriorate. For there is a human potential at its worst as well! And in spite of our belief in the

* Z. J. Lipowski, "The Conflict of Buridan's Ass, or Some Dilemmas of Affluence," *The American Journal of Psychiatry*, Vol. 127 (1970), pp. 49–55.

potential humanness of man we must not close our eyes to the fact that *humane* humans are, and probably will always remain, a minority. But it is precisely for this reason that each of us is challenged to *join* the minority. Things are bad. But unless we do our best to improve them, everything will become worse.

The will to meaning is not only a true manifestation of man's humanness, but also—as has been substantiated by Theodore A. Kotchen—a realiable criterion of mental health. This hypothesis is supported by James C. Crumbaugh, Sister Mary Raphael and Raymond R. Shrader, who measured the will to meaning and obtained the highest scores among well-motivated and successful professional and business populations.

On the other hand, lack of meaning and purpose is indicative of emotional maladjustment.* Since Freud and Adler had to deal with neurotic patients—that is to say, with people frustrated in their will to meaning—it is understandable that they thought that man is motivated by the pleasure principle and the striving for superiority, respectively. Actually, the will to power and what one might call a will to pleasure are substitutes for a frustrated will to meaning. Evidence of the surrogate nature of the will to pleasure has been offered by statistical research. People visiting Vienna's Prater—an amusement park somewhat comparable to New York's Coney Island —proved to be more frustrated in their will to meaning than the average population of Vienna.†

Primarily and normally man does not seek pleasure; instead, pleasure—or, for that matter, happiness—is the

---

* Elisabeth S. Lukas, Dissertation, University of Vienna, 1970.
† Elisabeth S. Lukas, *op. cit.*

side effect of living out the self-transcendence of existence. Once one has served a cause* or is involved in loving another human being, happiness occurs by itself. The will to pleasure, however, contradicts the self-transcendent quality of the human reality. And it also defeats itself. For pleasure and happiness are by-products. Happiness must ensue. It cannot be pursued. It is the very pursuit of happiness that thwarts happiness. The more one makes happiness an aim, the more he misses the aim. And this is most conspicious in cases of sexual neurosis such as frigidity or impotence. Sexual performance or experience is strangled to the extent to which it is made either an object of attention or an objective of intention. I have called the first "hyper-reflection" and the second "hyper-intention."

Hyper-intention is observable even on a mass level. Just consider the emphasis that public opinion places on sexual achievement. As I have pointed out elsewhere,† this emphasis spawns preoccupations and apprehensions. People are overly concerned with sexual success and ridden with the fear of sexual failure. But fear tends to bring about precisely that which one is afraid of. Thus a vicious circle is established. And it accounts for much of the case load regarding sexual neuroses which confronts psychiatrists today.

What is behind the emphasis on sexual achievement and power, what is behind this will to sexual pleasure and happiness is again the frustrated will to meaning. Sexual

---

* Albert Schweitzer once said, "The only ones among you who will be really happy are those who have sought and found how to serve."
† "Paradoxical Intention and De-reflection: Two Logotherapeutic Techniques," in Silvano Arieti and Gerard Chrzanowski, eds., *New Dimensions in Psychiatry* (New York: Wiley-Interscience, 1975).

libido only hypertrophies in an existential vacuum. The result is an inflation of sex; and like inflation on the money market, it is associated with a devaluation. More specifically, sex is devalued insofar as it is dehumanized. Because human sex is always more than mere sex.* And it is more than mere sex precisely to the extent that it serves as *the physical expression of something metasexual*—the physical expression of love. And only to the extent that sex carries out this function of embodying—incarnating—love, only to this extent will it climax in a truly rewarding experience. Seen in this light, Maslow was justified when he pointed out that those people who cannot love never get the same thrill out of sex as those who can love. Therefore we would have to recommend that sex be rehumanized if only for the purpose of maximizing one's orgasm. This was recently substantiated by a report on 20,000 responses to 101 questions about sexual attitudes and practices; it revealed that among the factors contributing to high orgasm and potency rates, the most important one was "romanticism."†

And yet it is not quite accurate to say that human sex is more than mere sex. As the ethologist Irenaeus Eibl-Eibesfeldt has shown, in some vertebrates sexual behavior serves group cohesion, and this is particularly the case

---

* Sometimes sex is also less than sex. William Simon and John Henry Gagnon contend that Freud went wrong in interpreting the sexuality of children with grown-up eyes. "It is dangerous to assume," the authors write, "that because some childhood behavior appears sexual to adults, it must be sexual." Parents who catch a young child playing with his genital organs will instinctively define the act as masturbation; to the child, the experience may well be a nonsexual experience of bodily discovery (*Time* Magazine, March 28, 1969).

† Robert Athanesiou, Phillip Shaver, and Carlo Tavris, "A *Psychology Today* Report on 20,000 Responses to 101 Questions about Sexual Attitudes and Practices," *Psychology Today*, Vol. 4 (1970), pp. 37–52.

in man's biological ancestors—those primates that live in groups; thus in certain apes sexual intercourse sometimes serves a social purpose exclusively; in humans, Eibl-Eibes-feldt states, there is no doubt that sexual intercourse not only serves the propagation of the species, but also the monogamous relation between the partners.

It goes without saying that the sexual instinct cannot in itself be distinctly human. After all, it is not only a property of human beings but is shared by animals as well. So let us more cautiously say that in man the sexual instinct is humanized to a higher or a lower degree, as the case may be; in him the sexual instinct approaches and approximates the potential of human sex only successively—and, as we have seen, the potential of human sex consists in its becoming an embodiment of love.

This sexual maturation is characterized by three developmental stages. The first two can be understood along the lines of Freud's differentiation between the goal of an instinct and the instinct's object. At the immature level, only a goal is sought, and the goal is tension reduction irrespective of the way in which it is accomplished. Masturbation may do. According to Freud the mature stage is reached as soon as the sexual instinct centers on the normal sexual intercourse which presupposes an object. As I see it, however, the object is not enough to guarantee a mature sexual life. For as long as an individual uses a partner simply for the purpose of reducing tension, he really "masturbates on the partner," as our patients so often say. To the individual who really is mature, the partner is in no way a means to an end. The mature individual's partnership moves on a human level, and the human level precludes the mere use of others. On the human level, I do not use another human being but I encounter him, which means that I fully recognize his humanness; and if I take another step by fully recognizing, beyond his humanness as a human being, his uniqueness as a person, it is even more than an encounter—what then takes place is love.*

Grasping the uniqueness of a partner understandably results in a monogamous partnership. There are no longer interchangeable partners. Conversely, if one is not able to love, he winds up with promiscuity. As masturbation means being content with tension reduction as a goal, so promiscuity means being contented with the partner as an object. In neither case is the human potential of sex actualized.

As long as one remains at the mere goal level, one's sexual instinct may be catered to by pornography; and as long as he stays at the mere object level his sexual instinct may be catered to by prostitutes. Thus, promiscuity and pornography are the marks of fixation at, or regression to, immature levels of development. Therefore it is not wise publicly to glorify the indulgence in such patterns of regressive behavior by confusing it with a progressive mentality. As to pornography, I detest the invocation of "freedom from censorship" when what is really meant is simply the freedom to make money. As compared with the hypocrisy of businessmen working in the field of so-called "sex education," I praise the honesty of the call girls who bluntly confess that they are only out to make money through sex. And as to promiscuity, it not only is a type of

* Once we recognize that uniqueness, personhood and selfhood really are interchangeable terms, we may say that the more one becomes himself, the more human he is. Cf. Viktor E. Frankl, "The Depersonalization of Sex," *Synthesis (The Realization of the Self)*, Vol. I, No. 1, (Spring 1974), pp. 7–11.

regressive behavior but also contradicts the humanness of man. But sexual promiscuity is promulgated together with sexual intimacy, and the latter is even believed to be the answer to the ills of our age. However, I think that what is needed in this age of population explosion is existential privacy rather than sexual intimacy.*

Speaking of population explosion, I would like to touch on the Pill. It is not only counteracting population explosion but, as I see it, rendering an even greater service. If it is true that it is love that makes sex human, the Pill allows for a truly human sexual life, one in which, freed from its automatic connection with procreation, sex can realize its highest potential as one of the most direct and meaningful expressions of love. Sex is human if it is experienced as a vehicle of love; and to make it into a mere means to an end contradicts the humanness of sex, regardless of whether the pleasure principle dictates the end or the procreation instinct does so. As to the latter, sex has been emancipated, thanks to the Pill, and has thereby become capable of achieving its potential status as a human phenomenon.

Today the will to meaning is often frustrated. In logotherapy one speaks of existential frustration. We psychiatrists are confronted more than ever before with patients who are complaining of a *feeling of futility* which at present plays at least as important a role as did the *feeling of inferiority* in Alfred Adler's time. Let me just quote from a letter I recently received from a young American student: "I am a 22-year-old with degree, car,

* Cf. Viktor E. Frankl, "Encounter: The Concept and Its Vulgarization," *The Journal of the American Academy of Psychoanalysis*, Vol. I, No. 1 (1973), pp. 73–83.

security and the availability of more sex and power than I need. Now I have only to explain to myself what it all means." However, such people are complaining not only of a sense of meaninglessness but also of emptiness, and that is why I have described this condition in terms of the "existential vacuum."

There is no doubt that the existential vacuum is increasing and spreading. According to a report I was shown recently, the percentage of those suffering from it, among a population of 500 Viennese youngsters, has increased within the last two years from 30 percent to 80 percent. Even in Africa the existential vacuum is spreading, particularly among the academic youth.* Also, Freudians are fully aware of this phenomenon, and so are Marxists. At an international meeting of psychoanalysts it was stated that ever more patients are suffering from a lack of life content, rather than clinical symptomatology, and that this state of affairs may well account for so-called interminable analyses because, as the Freudians have contended, in such cases the psychoanalytic treatment becomes the only life content available to the patient. As to the Marxists, only recently the head of the department of psychotherapy at Karl Marx University in Leipzig confessed to the frequency of the existential vacuum as substantiated by her own investigations. As the head of the psychiatry department at a Czech university puts it, the existential vacuum is passing the borders between capitalist and Communist countries "without a visa."†

---

* Louis L. Klitzke, "Students in Emerging Africa: Humanistic Psychology and Logotherapy in Tanzania" in American Journal of Humanistic Psychology, Vol. 9 (1969), pp. 105–26.
† Osvald Vymetal, Acta Universitatis Palackiannae, Vol. 13 (1966), pp. 265–88.

If asked for a brief explanation, I would say that the existential vacuum derives from the following conditions. Unlike an animal, man is no longer told by drives and instincts what he must do. And in contrast to man in former times, he is no longer told by traditions and values what he should do. Now, knowing neither what he must do nor what he should do, he sometimes does not even know what he basically wishes to do. Instead, he wishes to do what other people do—which is conformism—or he does what other people wish him to do—which is totalitarianism.

In addition to these two effects of the existential vacuum, there is a third, namely, neuroticism. Per se, the existential vacuum is not a neurosis, at least not in the strictly clinical sense. If it is a neurosis at all it would have to be diagnosed as a *sociogenic neurosis*. However, there are also cases in which the existential vacuum results in clinical symptomatology. Such patients are suffering from what I have called "noögenic neuroses." James C. Crumbaugh must be credited with having developed a special diagnostic test to differentiate the noögenic from other forms of neurosis. Scores of research projects have been based on his PIL Test. The results thereby obtained indicate that about 20 percent of the neuroses one encounters are noögenic in nature and origin. Elisabeth S. Lukas, although using a different test (her Logo-Test), has arrived at the same percentage as Crumbaugh.

As to the existential vacuum, however, which in itself is not a neurosis, a statistical survey recently showed that among my European students, 25 percent had themselves had this "abyss experience," as it may be called in contradistinction to the "peak experience." Among my American students it was not 25 but 60 percent.

A Communist psychiatrist found that among various populations of Czech students the percentage of those who had experienced the existential vacuum as measured by Crumbaugh's test was even higher than that observed and reported among students in the United States. A year later, however, the figure had become markedly lower. During that intervening year, most of the students had become involved in Dubček's movement, his battle for political liberalization and for the humanization of communism. They had been given a cause for which to fight, for which to live and, unfortunately, also to die.

On the average, however, the fact remains that in America the existential vacuum is more manifest than in Europe. As I see it, this is due to the exposure of the average American student to an indoctrination along the lines of reductionism. To cite an instance, there is a book in which man is defined as "nothing but a complex biochemical mechanism powered by a combustion system which energizes computers with prodigious storage facilities for retaining encoded information." Or, to quote another example, man is defined as a "naked ape." By offering our students such reductionist concepts of man we are reinforcing their existential vacuum. I well remember how I felt when I was a thirteen-year-old junior-high-school student and our natural-science teacher told us that life in the final analysis was "nothing but a combustion process, an oxidation process." I sprang to my feet and said, "Professor, if this is the case, what meaning then does life have?" To be sure, in his case reductionism had taken on the form of "oxidationism," one might say.

A study of physicians by R. N. Gray and associates ("An Analysis of Physicians' Attitudes of Cynicism and Humanitarianism before and after Entering Medical Practice," *Journal of Medical Education*, 40 [1955], p. 760) showed that during medical school cynicism as a rule increases, while humanitarianism decreases. Only after completion of medical studies is this trend reversed, but unfortunately not in all subjects. Small wonder, I would say. Just consider the two definitions offered by the author in whose paper this study was quoted. Man is defined as nothing but "an adaptive control system," and values are defined as nothing but "homeostatic restraints in a stimulus-response process" (Joseph Wilder, "Values and Psychotherapy," *American Journal of Psychotherapy*, 23 [1969], p. 405). According to another reductionist definition, values are nothing but reaction formations and defense mechanisms. As for myself, I am not prepared to live for the sake of my reaction formations, even less to die for the sake of my defense mechanisms.

Here is another illustration regarding reductionism. A famous Freudian psychoanalyst devoted two volumes to Goethe. "In the 1,538 pages," a review of the book reads, "the author portrays to us a genius with the earmarks of a manic-depressive, paranoid, and epileptoid disorder, of homosexuality, incest, voyeurism, exhibitionism, fetishism, impotence, narcissism, obsessive-compulsive neurosis, hysteria, megalomania, etc. He seems to focus almost exclusively upon the instinctual dynamic forces that underlie the artistic product. We are led to believe that Goethe's work is but the result of pregenital fixations. His struggle does not really aim for an ideal, for beauty, for values, but for the overcoming of an embarrassing problem of premature ejaculation" (the book review was published by Julius Heuscher in the *Journal of Existentialism*, 5 [1964], p. 229). How wise and cautious was Freud, as compared with his epigones, when he remarked that sometimes a cigar may be a cigar and nothing but a cigar. To be sure, a Freudian would have to interpret Freud's statement as a rationalization of his cigar smoking.

The reductionist interpretation of values is likely to undermine and erode the enthusiasm of youth. As an example, let me report the following observation. A young American couple who had served as Peace Corps volunteers in Africa returned completely fed up and disgusted. At the outset they had had to participate in mandatory group sessions led by a psychologist who played a game somewhat as follows:

"Why did you join the Peace Corps?"

"We wanted to help people less privileged."

"So you must be superior to them."

"In a way."

"So there must be in you, in your unconscious, a need to prove to yourself that you are superior."

"Well, we never thought of it that way, but you are a psychologist, you certainly know better."

And so it went on. They were indoctrinated in the interpretation of their idealism and altruism as mere personal hang-ups. Even worse, they "were constantly on each other's backs, playing the 'what's *your* hidden motive' game," according to their report.

For a long time psychoanalysis has understood itself in terms of a depth psychology, and depth psychology in turn has seen its assignment as the "unmasking" of unconscious dynamics underlying human behavior. Perhaps this is best illustrated by what Joseph Wilder once called the shortest psychiatric joke he ever had encountered:

"Are you a psychiatrist?"

"Why do you ask?"

"You're a psychiatrist."

By the very attempt to unmask the man who had asked him a question, the psychiatrist really unmasked himself. Now, unmasking is perfectly legitimate; but I would say that it must stop as soon as one confronts what is genuine, genuinely human, in man. If it does not stop there, the only thing that the "unmasking psychologist" really unmasks is his own "hidden motive"—namely, his unconscious need to debase and depreciate the humanness of man.

At that point hyper-interpretation, as I would call it, begins, and it proves to be most dangerous when it comes to self-interpretation. We psychiatrists have met many patients who are suffering from, and crippled by, the obsessive compulsion to analyze themselves, to observe and watch themselves, to reflect upon themselves. The cultural climate that prevails in the United States provides dangerous opportunity for this compulsion to become a *collective obsessive neurosis.* Just consider a recent study by Edith Weisskopf-Joelson and associates ("Relative Emphasis on Nine Values by a Group of College Students," *Psychological Report,* 24 [1969] p. 299). It shows that the value that ranks highest among American college students is self-interpretation.* I see in these findings another indication of the existential vacuum. As the boomerang returns to the hunter who has thrown it only when it has missed its target, so man returns to himself, reflects upon himself and becomes overly concerned with self-interpretation only when he has, as it were, missed his mission, having been frustrated in his search

* The value that ranks next to self-interpretation is self-actualization. Ultimately, however, man can actualize himself only by fulfilling a meaning out in the world, rather than within himself, and self-actualization is available only as an effect of self-transcendence.

for meaning. The Freudians' experience with patients in whom, owing to the lack of life content, the psychoanalytic treatment has become a substitute comes to mind.

Now let us turn from the causes to the effects of the existential vacuum, inasmuch as these go beyond both the noögenic neurosis and the feeling of meaninglessness which is to be diagnosed as a sociogenic neurosis. Among the worldwide effects there is something one might call the *mass neurotic triad,* and it consists of *depression, addiction* and *aggression.* When I once took a taxi to a university whose student body had invited me to give a lecture on the question of whether "the new generation is mad," I asked the cab driver to answer it. He came up with the following succinct statement: "Of course they are mad; they kill themselves, they kill each other, and they take dope."

As to the first aspect of this triad, depression results in suicide, and there is ample evidence that, particularly among the young generation, the number of suicides is increasing. "Suicide, which once ranked twenty-second on the list of causes of death in the United States, now rates tenth, and in some states, sixth. And for everyone who succeeds in committing suicide, fifteen will have tried and failed." (Earl A. Grollman, *Concerning Death: A Practical Guide for the Living* [Boston: Beacon Press, 1974].) What is even more important, "suicide rates among young people have risen dramatically. While suicide is listed as the tenth leading cause of death in the United States, it is third now among youth fifteen to nineteen years old, and second among college students."

The spreading existential frustration lies at the root of this phenomenon. In fact, a study conducted at Idaho State University revealed that 51 of 60 students (85 percent) who had seriously attempted suicide reported as the reason that "life meant nothing" to them. Of these 51, 48 (93 percent) were in excellent physical health, were actively engaged socially, were performing well academically, and were on good terms with their family groups. (Vann A. Smith, personal communication.)

In this context I would like to quote also from a letter an American medical student recently wrote to me: "All around me here in the U.S. I see young people my age who are desperately groping for a meaning to their existence. One of my best friends died as a result of his search. I know now that if he were here now I could help him, thanks to your book, but he is not. His death, however, will always serve to pull me toward all people who are in distress. I think this is the most powerful motivation anyone can have. I have found a meaning (despite my deep sorrow and guilt) in my friend's life and death. If I can be strong enough in the future as a medical doctor to do my job and fulfill my responsibility, his death will not have been in vain. I want more than anything to prevent this tragedy from happening to others."

Small wonder that people who are caught in the existential vacuum are eager, if meanings cannot be acquired, to provide themselves at least with mere *feelings* of meaningfulness—such as those that are available in that state of intoxication which is induced by LSD. In such states suddenly the world takes on infinite meaningfulness. But the short cut finally proves to be a dead end, for it might well be that people who resort to LSD wind up in the long run as those animals did which were used by Olds and Milner in the course of self-stimulation experiments. They inserted electrodes into the hypothalamuses of rats, and whenever they closed the electric circuit the rats to all appearances experienced either sexual orgasm or the satisfaction of the ingestion of food. When the rats then learned to jump on the lever and by so doing to close the electric circuit themselves, they became addicted to the business and pressed the lever up to 50,000 times a day. What I regard as most remarkable is that these animals then neglected the real sexual partners and the real food that were offered to them. And I think that the "acid heads" who confine themselves to the mere feelings of meaningfulness may bypass the true meanings which are in store, in wait for them, to be fulfilled by them out there in the world rather than within their own psyches.

Since I advanced this hypothesis regarding the real source from which the drug scene derives, numerous authors have written about the feeling of meaninglessness of life as it is reported by young people involved with drugs. This at least is the contention of Betty Lou Padelford, who devoted a dissertation to "The Influence of Ethnic Background, Sex, and Father Image upon the Relationship Between Drug Involvement and Purpose in Life" (United States International University, San Diego, January 1973). As Dr. Padelford points out, "The lack of a strong father figure with whom the young male could identify was felt by many authorities to be a precondition to illicit drug involvement." However, the data generated by her own study "*failed* to identify significant differences between the extent of drug involvement reported by students having a weak father image as opposed to students having a strong father image." The subjects studied in her investigation were 416 students, and a significant relationship between drug involvement and purpose in life was found beyond reasonable doubt ($r = -.23$; $p < .001$). The mean drug-involvement index for students with low purpose in life (8.90) was found to differ significantly from the mean drug-involvement index for students with high purpose in life (4.25).

Dr. Padelford also reviews the literature in the field which, along with her own research, confirms the existential vacuum hypothesis. Nowlis addressed the question of why students were interested in and took drugs. Among the reasons often listed was "the desire to find meaning in life." One of the epidemiological studies conducted for the National Commission on Marijuana and Drug Abuse was a survey of 455 students in the San Diego area, made by Judd et al. Users of both marijuana and hallucinogens indicated they were bothered by and had suffered over the lack of meaning of life more than had nonusers. Another study reported in the literature was conducted by Mirin et al., who found that heavy use was correlated with search for meaningful experience and diminished goal-directed activity. Linn surveyed 700 undergraduates at the University of Wisconsin, Milwaukee, in 1968 and reported that marijuana users, compared with nonusers, were more concerned about the meaning of life. Krippner et al. theorized that drug usage may be a form of self-administered psychotherapy for people with existential problems, e.g., the 100 percent positive response to "Have things seemed meaningless to you?" Shean and Fechtman ("Purpose in Life Scores of Student Marihuana Users," *Journal of Clinical Psychology*, 27 [1971], pp. 112–13) found that students who had smoked marijuana regularly over a six-month period scored significantly lower ($p <$ .001) on Crumbaugh's Purpose-in-Life Test than did the nonusers.

In another area, i.e., the addiction to alcohol, parallel findings were published by, among others, Annemarie

Von Forstmeyer, who has shown in a dissertation that 18 out of 20 alcoholics looked upon their existence as meaningless and without purpose (United States International University, 1970). Accordingly, logotherapeutically oriented techniques proved superior to other forms of therapy. James C. Crumbaugh ("Changes in Frankl's Existential Vacuum as a Measure of Therapeutic Outcome," *Newsletter for Research in Psychology*, 14 [1972], pp. 35–37) measured existential vacuum to compare the outcome of group logotherapy with results achieved by an alcoholic treatment unit and a marathon therapy program. "Only logotherapy showed a statistically significant improvement." That logotherapy equally lends itself to the treatment of drug addiction has been shown by Alvin R. Fraiser at the Narcotic Addict Rehabilitation Center at Norco, California. From 1966 to the present, the approach he has used in working with narcotic addicts has been logotherapy. "As a result of this approach," he says, "I have become the only counselor in the history of the institution to have three consecutive years of the highest success rate (success meaning that the addict is not returned to the institution within one year after release). My approach to dealing with the addict has resulted in a three-year 40 percent success rate as compared to an institutional average of about 11 percent (using the established approach)."

As to the last aspect of the triad, aggression, for too long a time research in human behavior has been based on a mechanistic concept of aggression. This approach still adheres to an old-fashioned, out-dated motivation theory that depicts man as a being to whom the world ultimately serves as a mere tool for the reduction of the tensions aroused and created by libidinal or aggressive impulses.

However, in contrast to this closed-system concept, man is actually a being who is reaching out for meanings to fulfill and other human beings to encounter. And certainly these fellow beings, his partners, mean more to him than just a means to the end of living out his aggressive and sexual drives and instincts. However, regarding the alternative to living them out—that is, the possibility of sublimating them—Carolyn Wood Sherif has warned us of the dangers of harboring an illusion that is so characteristic of all the closed-system concepts of man, namely, the illusion that aggression can be drained by being turned to harmless activities, such as sports ("Intergroup Conflict and Competition: Social-Psychological Analysis," paper presented to Scientific Congress, XX Olympic Games, Munich, August 22, 1972, at plenary session on Sport and Conflict). On the contrary, "there is a substantial body of research evidence that the successful execution of aggressive actions, far from reducing subsequent aggression, is the best way to increase the frequency of aggressive responses (such studies have included both animal and human behavior)."

Fredrick Wertham, in his "Critique of the Report to the Surgeon General from The Committee on Television and Social Behavior" (*American Journal of Psychotherapy*, 26 [1972], p. 216), ridicules "the old getting-rid-of-aggression notion" according to which "we 'need' TV violence to relieve violent impulses and thus 'spare us real violence.' Clinical studies have revealed the adverse effects on children and youth of television violence, brutality, and sadism. TV violence was found in hundreds of cases to have harmful effects." The President's Commission on the Causes and Prevention of Violence also stated that the "constant diet of violent behavior on television has an adverse effect on human character and attitudes." "Reduction of violence in entertainment media would," therefore, "be of benefit," says Jerome D. Frank ("Some Psychological Determinants of Violence and Its Control," *Aust. N. Z. Psychiatry,* 6 [1972], pp. 158–64). And in *The British Journal of Psychiatry* (Vol. 122, No. 566 [1973], pp 53–56), an experiment is described in whose course "children were shown films portraying aggressive acts," and in fact, "increases in aggression occurred consistently over and above the initial tendency to behave in that way" (Bromley H. Kniveton and Geoffrey M. Stephenson, "An Examination of Individual Susceptibility to the Influence of Aggressive Film Models"). John P. Murray (National Institute of Mental Health) summarizes the results of "a number of studies as follows: viewing televised violence causes the viewer to become more aggressive" ("Television and Violence," *American Psychologist,* 28 [1973], pp. 472–78).

Again, upon closer investigation, one may find that not only sexual libido thrives in an existential vacuum, but also aggressive "destrudo." Statistical evidence is favorable to my hypothesis that people are most likely to become aggressive when they are caught in this feeling of emptiness and meaninglessness. Robert Jay Lifton seems to agree with me when stating that "men are most apt to kill when they feel overcome by meaninglessness."* According to the research conducted by W. A. M. Black and R. A. M. Gregson, recidivists (96.80) differ significantly from first-sentence prisoners (99.07), who in turn differ from normals (115.07) with respect to pur-

---

* *History and Human Survival* (New York: Random House, 1969).

pose in life (p < 0.0005). The authors conclude that "criminality and purpose in life are inversely related. The irony is that the more persistently a man offends, the more likely he is to be sentenced to increasing terms of imprisonment and the less likely he is to increase his sense of purpose in life, and so the more likely he is to continue offending when released." ("Time Perspective, Purpose in Life, Extraversion and Neuroticism in New Zealand Prisoners," *British Journal of Social and Clinical Psychology*, 12 [1973], pp. 50–60.)

In the light of such facts it is understandable that Louis S. Barber holds that logotherapy is "particularly applicable to the treatment of juvenile delinquents." For several years he has worked with young people in a rehabilitation setting. Almost always the "lack of meaning and purpose in their lives" appeared to be present. "We have one of the highest rehabilitation rates in the U.S.," Barber says, "a recidivism rate of less than 17 percent (against an average of some 40 percent)." This program "builds responsibility within each of the boys. It is logo-education in practice." That "a logotherapeutic approach offers great possibilities to the field of rehabilitation" is evidenced by a mean increase in the will to meaning from 86.13 to 103.46 (within four months, at that) among the juvenile delinquents who were subject to Dr. Barber's treatment.

How, then, can psychotherapy at large cope with the mass neurotic triad: how can it tackle depression, addiction and aggression as they afflict mankind? If we include in the pathology of humanity what really is not neurosis in the strictly clinical sense but, rather, a para-clinical phenomenon, we are justified in speaking of a neuroticization of humanity. Now, it is my contention that the *de-neuroticization of humanity* requires a *re-humanization of psychotherapy*.

If one is to overcome the ills and ailments of this age, he must properly understand them—that is to say, understand them as the effects of frustration. And if one is to understand the frustrations of man, he has to understand his motivations, to begin with, and especially the most human of human motivations, which is man's search for meaning. This, however, is not possible unless psychotherapy detaches itself from its own reductionism. Everything short of a rehumanized psychotherapy would reinforce the mass neurotic triad. Consider the three aspects of reductionism—subjectivism, homeostasis and pandeterminism—and let us ask ourselves: If meanings and values really are "nothing but" defense mechanisms and reaction formations, as the psychodynamically oriented theories have it, is life really worth living? Isn't it rather understandable if I am submerged in depression and wind up with suicide? As to addiction: If man really is just seeking pleasure and happiness by gratifying his needs in order to get rid of the tensions created by them, why worry? Why not build up perpetual and perfect tranquility by simply taking drugs? And finally, regarding aggression: If I really am the victim of outer and inner circumstances and influences, the product of environment and heredity, and my behavior, decision and action are "nothing but" the result of operant conditioning, conditioned reflexes and learning processes—who is justified in demanding that I improve or expecting that I change? There is no need for apologies; there are plenty of excuses; there are alibis. And as for myself, I am neither free nor responsible. So there is no reason why I should not continue living out the aggressive impulses about which I can do nothing anyway.

From all this it should be clear that we are in dire need of a rehumanization of psychotherapy unless we wish to reinforce, rather than to counteract, the ills and ailments of our age. So let us briefly review the path that psychotherapy has taken since the time of Freud, with a view to an exploration of the factors that are likely to account for a dehumanization of psychotherapy.

Freud's psychoanalysis teaches how to *unmask the neurotic*; how to determine the hidden, unconscious dynamics underlying his behavior. This behavior is "analyzed," and analyzing in this context means interpreting. Later on, however, the assumption of the unconscious was "used as a carte blanche on which almost any causal explanation could be written," to quote from a paper published in *Psychology Today*. Explanatory devices, some skeptical therapists argued, "as often as not actually cover up rather than reveal the empirical data."

In contradistinction, and counteraction, to the psychoanalytic system, Carl Rogers' approach to counseling is characterized by restraint from being directive and abstention from interpretations. After all, interpretation along the lines of the psychoanalytic system is based on free associations. However, they are "never truly 'free,' " to quote Judd Marmor. They rather are influenced by the analysts, and the patients are indoctrinated in a very specific *Weltanschauung* or ideology. According to the particularly Freudian psychoanalytic ideology, man is ultimately nothing but a being ruled and governed by the homeostasis principle; human love is nothing but the expression of a sublimated and aim-inhibited sexual drive;

and as for personal conscience, that is no more than one's superego or the introjection of his father image. It is in this area that Rogers' principal merit lies, for I would say that it is to his credit to have shown us how to *de-ideologize psychotherapy*.

Moreover, "in the past ten years the prestige of psychoanalysis has dropped significantly in academic and scientific circles," again to quote from Marmor, because "over the years psychoanalysis has been oversold as an optimal psychotherapeutic technique. Whether or not classical psychoanalysis is truly the optimal approach for any specific form of psychopathology still remains to be conclusively proved," Marmor believes, since "at best it is indicated in only a small proportion of cases." ("The Current Status of Psychoanalysis in American Psychiatry," *American Journal of Psychiatry*, 125 [1968], pp. 131–32.)

Of course; the question may be asked why psychoanalysis still "is in a position to perpetuate its theories, proven or unproven," and T. P. Millar offers the following explanation:

The voice of dissent is not easily heard in psychiatric America. We are in an era when the *sine qua non* of publication in many a psychiatric journal is a dynamic formulation of the problem in oral, anal or Oedipal terms. We are in an era when to disagree with psychoanalysis is more liable to lead to a gratuitous diagnosis and dynamic formulation of the disagreer than it is to an examination of the arguments advanced. Indeed, by diagnosing the opposition, the ideas advanced are rendered grist for the interpretative mill rather than propositions to be refuted. But can it be that only psychoanalysts have *opinions* while the rest of us have *problems*? Dr. Burness Moore, chairman of the American Psychoanalytic Association's public information committee, writes in that Association's newsletter:

"Indeed, there is indication of increasing derogation of analysis in the past few years," and the Association has hired a public relations consultant.

"This," Millar comments, "may indeed be the appropriate action, but it does seem possible that more might be accomplished if psychoanalysis were to undertake to rehabilitate its theory rather than its public image." ("Who's Afraid of Sigmund Freud?" *British Journal of Psychiatry*, 115 [1969], pp. 421–28.)

However, psychoanalysis had already lost much of its territory to a sound and sober trend in the field of psychotherapy, namely, behavior therapy. As early as 1960, H. J. Eysenck deplored "the lack of experimental or clinical evidence in favor of psychoanalysis." The theories of psychoanalysis are "beliefs" with which "psychiatrists in training are now frequently indoctrinated." However, Eysenck argues not only in general that "Freudian theories are outside the realm of science" but also in particular that "so-called symptomatic cures can be achieved which are long-lasting and do not produce alternative symptoms." This fact "argues strongly against the Freudian hypothesis." In contrast to the Freudian "belief," Eysenck thinks that abolition of the symptoms does not at all "leave behind some mysterious complex seeking outlet in alternative symptoms." (*Behavior Therapy and the Neuroses* [New York: Pergamon Press, 1960].)

Long before this, logotherapy also had offered evidence that neuroses need not in each and every case be traced to the Oedipal situation or other types of conflicts and complexes but may derive from feedback mechanisms such as the circle formation built up by anticipatory anxiety (cf. Viktor E. Frankl, *"Zur medikamentö-sen Unterstützung der Psychotherapie bei Neurosen,"* Schweizer Archiv für Neurologie und Psychiatrie, 43 [1939], pp. 26–31). And as early as 1947 I myself attempted to interpret neurosis in reflexological terms when pointing out that "all psychoanalytically oriented psycho-therapies are mainly concerned with uncovering the primary conditions of the 'conditioned reflex,' which neurosis can be understood to be, and 'the primary conditions' are represented by the situation—outer and inner—in which a given neurotic symptom emerged for the first time. It is my contention, however, that the full-fledged neurosis is not only caused by the *primary conditions* but also by *secondary conditioning.* This *reinforcement,* in turn, is caused by the feedback mechanism called antici-patory anxiety. Therefore, if we wish to *recondition* a conditioned reflex, we must break the vicious cycle formed by anticipatory anxiety, and this is the very job done by the logotherapeutic 'paradoxical intention' technique." (*Die Psychotherapie in der Praxis* [Vienna: Franz Deuticke, 1947].)

It is my contention that behavior therapy has made a valuable contribution to the evolution of psychotherapy in that it has shown how to *de-mythologize neurosis.* This formulation is not too farfetched when one considers the fact that Sigmund Freud himself described his instinct theory as a "mythology" and the instincts as "mythical" entities.

To sum up, Freud has unmasked the neurotic; Rogers has de-ideologized psychotherapy; and Eysenck, Wolpe and others have de-mythologized neurosis; and yet a dis-content remained. Even to such a declared materialist as Christa Kohler, who runs the department of psychotherapy at Karl Marx University in Leipzig, East Germany, "the behavioristically oriented psychotherapists Wolpe and Eysenck" are, to her mind, excessively "sliding into a biologistic and mechanistic position." (*"Der Einfluss des Menschenbildes auf die Neurosentheorie,"* in L. Pickenhain and A. Thom, eds., *Beiträg zu einer allgemeinen Theorie der Psychiatrie* [Jena: Fischer, 1968].) She may be right. Particularly in an era such as ours, one of meaninglessness, depersonalization and dehumanization, it is not possible to cope with the ills of the age unless the human dimension, the dimension of human phenomena, is included in the concept of man which indispensably underlies every sort of psychotherapy, be it on the conscious or unconscious level.

Nikolaus Petrilowitsch of the department of psychiatry at the University of Mainz, West Germany, has drawn attention to the fact that logotherapy—in contrast to all other schools of psychotherapy—does not remain in the dimension of neurosis. What does he mean? Psychoanalysis sees in neurosis the result of certain psychodynamics which it counteracts by bringing into play, say, transference, which, to be sure, is another sort of psychodynamics. And as to behavior therapy, it sees neurosis as the result of conditioning, of certain learning processes, and counteracts these by means of reconditioning processes, relearning. But logotherapy, as Petrilowitsch sees it, goes beyond the plane of neurosis and opens up the dimension of the human phenomena, thereby placing itself in a position to tap and draw upon the resources that are available in this dimension—resources such as the uniquely human capacities of self-transcendence and what I have come to call "self-detachment."

Petrilowitsch now credits logotherapy for having *re-*

*humanized psychotherapy** so that, after the unmasking of the neurotic, after the de-ideologizing of psychotherapy and the de-mythologizing of neurosis, the re-humanizing of psychotherapy has been arrived at, or at least is under way.

But now let us come back for a moment to the two uniquely human capacities of self-transcendence and self-detachment. The latter signifies the capacity to detach oneself from oneself. Paradoxical intention—a logotherapeutic technique that lends itself to the short-term treatment of obsessive-compulsive and phobic neuroses—is intended to muster and mobilize self-detachment in general. In particular, however, it utilizes a unique and specific aspect of self-detachment, namely, the human sense of humor. Small wonder that, by methodologically including this important facet of man's humanness in its armamentarium, logotherapy acquires an additional asset over behavior therapy. This does not detract from the fact that techniques which parallel paradoxical intention are applied and used in behavior modification. But it is remarkable and noteworthy that Dr. Iver Hand of London's Maudsley Hospital found that patients who had been treated along the lines of behavior therapy in a group setting "used humor spontaneously as one of their main coping mechanisms." (Paper read at the Symposium on Logotherapy, sponsored by the American Psychological Association, 1973.) Other behavioristically oriented authors such as L. Solyom, J. Garza-Perez, B. L. Ledwidge

---

* Petrilowitsch really spoke in this context of its having "re-humanized *psychoanalysis*," but in addition to the statement made by Petrilowitsch, there is a similar one made by the Norwegian learning theorist and behavior therapist Bjarne Kvilhaug to the effect that "logotherapy has re-humanized *learning theory*."

and C. Solyom* not only successfully applied paradoxical intention but also offered statistical and even experimental evidence that it really works, and that the therapeutic results obtained by this logotherapeutic technique cannot be dismissed as the effects of mere suggestion.†

By and large, obsessive-compulsive and phobic neuroses are psychogenic as opposed to noögenic, so one may say that invoking the human potential of self-detachment is instrumental in the therapy of psychogenic neuroses. Cognizance of self-transcendence, however, is indispensable in the diagnosis of noögenic neuroses. The noögenic neurosis is the effect of a frustration of the will to meaning, which in turn is a manifestation of self-transcendence.

Self-transcendence and self-detachment are irreducibly human phenomena and exclusively available in the human dimension. From this it follows that we cannot really help man in his predicament if we insist that our concept of man be patterned after the "machine model" or after the "rat model," as Gordon W. Allport mockingly put it. After all, there are no computers that laugh about themselves, nor are there animals that care about meaning and purpose in their existence.

The engineering approach to the patient, as a machine to repair or a mechanism to fix, may by itself be detrimental. It may debilitate the patient's awareness of himself as a free and responsible agent. In other words, it may eventuate in an iatrogenic neurosis—a neurosis, that

* "Paradoxical Intention in the Treatment of Obsessional Thoughts: A Pilot Study," *Comprehensive Psychiatry*, Vol. 13, No. 3 (May 1972), pp. 291–97.
† Also see Viktor E. Frankl, "Paradoxical Intention: A Logotherapeutic Technique," in Harold Greenwald, ed., *Active Psychotherapy* (New York: Atherton Press, 1967).

is, which is caused by the physician. As in this case the doctor is a psychiatrist, one might speak of a *psychiatrogenic neurosis*. The psychotherapist must therefore reexamine the philosophical underpinnings of whatever approach he adopts, lest he inflict such a psychiatrogenic neurosis on the patient. This is the reason why logotherapy is not only a successful therapeutic procedure in noögenic, sociogenic and psychogenic cases but also a prophylactic measure with respect to the psychiatrogenic neuroses.

We have heard that man is a being in search of meaning. We have seen that today his search is unsatisfied and that this constitutes the pathology of our age. The time has come to ask ourselves, What is the therapy? In order to answer this question, we must focus first on another one: namely, how does this meaning-seeking being search for meaning, and also, how does he manage to find it? There is no doubt that meaning must be found and cannot be given. Least of all can it be given by us psychiatrists. We must be satisfied if our colleagues do not take away their patients' meaning and purpose. For example, I recently received a letter which contained the following passage: "I have had recurrent depressive states until two days ago a psychiatrist at Harvard University (where I am a student) told me bluntly . . . 'your life is meaningless, you have nothing to look forward to, I am surprised that you haven't committed suicide.' " Is this enough to do? Is that all a psychiatrist has to offer? I do not think so. Or, to cite an instance to which Edith Weisskopf-Joelson of the University of Georgia drew attention: "A woman suffering from an incurable cancer was comparing the fullness of her previous life with the senselessness of the ultimate phase. Thereupon a Freudian psychoanalyst countered that he believed she had made a gross mistake. 'Her life-in-general had been without meaning even before the onset of her disease. In reality, the two phases were bare of meaning and sense.'" ("Some Suggestions Concerning the Concept of Awareness," *Psychotherapy*, 8 [1971], pp. 2–7.)

To repeat, meaning must be found and cannot be given. To give meanings would amount to moralizing. But I for one think that if morals are to survive they will have to be ontologized. Ontologized morals, however, will no longer define what is good and what is bad in terms of what one should do and what one must not do. What is good will be defined as that which fosters the meaning fulfillment of a being. And what is bad will be defined as that which hinders this meaning fulfillment.

To say that meaning must be found is equivalent to saying that meaning is something to discover rather than to invent. This in turn is equivalent to saying that the "demand characteristics" (Kurt Lewin) or "demand qualities" inherent in a given situation, the "requirements" of the situation, are "objective qualities." (Max Wertheimer, "Some Problems in the Theory of Ethics," in M. Henle, ed., *Documents of Gestalt Psychology* [Berkeley: University of California Press, 1961].) Thus meanings prove to be objective, rather than merely subjective, on empirical grounds.

Consider the situation of a subject confronted with a Rorschach test: he is reading into the ink blots an entirely subjective meaning—a meaning whose very subjectiveness betrays the makeup of his personality, as is the case in any "projective" test. But life, I would say, does not compare to a Rorschach test but, rather, to what is called an "embedded figure." Here one cannot simply read "a" meaning into the drawing but must find out "the" meaning which is objectively there, even though it is hidden and therefore still to be discovered.

James C. Crumbaugh must be credited with having shown that the discovery of meaning has something to do with a gestalt perception. The will to meaning, he writes, "can be comprehended in terms of the Gestalt psychologists' laws of perceptual organization," and he "relates it to perception—the will to perceive, to read meaning into the environment, to interpret and organize stimulus elements into meaningful wholes."

The Gestalt psychologists hold this organizational tendency to be an innate property of the mind. It has survival value, for the greater the range of stimuli which can be comprehended and interrelated, the greater the chance of adaptive manipulation. By the will to meaning, however, Frankl implies a particular kind of perception: Man not only strives to perceive his environment as a meaningful totality, but he strives to find an interpretation which will reveal him as an individual with a purpose to fulfill in order to complete this total Gestalt—he strives to find an *apologia pro vita sua*, a justification for his existence. The Gestalt laws of organization, subsumed under the law of *Prägnanz*, or filledness, represent an unlearned striving to construct meaningful, unified Gestalten from all elements of experience. Frankl's will to meaning can be considered another way of looking at the same concept, though there is an advantage in his thinking, for it is a particularly human idea, pointing up man's distinctive ability to perceive or find meaning not merely in what is, but in what can be. This is the ability which Max Scheler has called the capacity for free contemplation of the possible, and which he considers the factor that separates man from the lower animals.

Crumbaugh concludes by pointing out that "evidence favorable to Frankl's postulated drive would be found in the accumulated evidence of the Gestalt leaders, principally Koffka and Köhler, for the Gestalt laws of organization. As previously noted, the will to meaning is primarily a perceptual phenomenon. It follows that if innate tendencies toward perceptual organization exist, it may be claimed that they manifest a striving toward organization of experience into ontologically significant patterns." ("The Validation of Logotherapy," in R. M. Jurjevich, ed., *Direct Psychotherapy* [Coral Gables, Fla.: University of Miami Press, 1973].)

So meaning must be found and cannot be given. And it must be found by oneself, by one's own conscience. Conscience may be defined as a means to discover meanings, to "sniff them out," as it were. In fact, conscience lets us arrive at the unique meaning gestalts dormant in all the unique situations which form a string called a man's life. Insofar as the perception of such meaning gestalts boils down to the interpretation of given life situations, Karl Barth was right when he said that "conscience is the true interpreter of life." And if we now ask ourselves by what man is led and guided in his search for meaning, certainly this function is carried out by conscience.

Conscience is a human phenomenon, and we must first of all see to it that it is preserved in its humanness rather than being dealt with reductionistically. Reductionism is a pseudo-scientific procedure that either reduces human phenomena to, or deduces them from, subhuman phenomena. For example, conscience is reductionistically interpreted as nothing but the result of conditioning processes. But the behavior of a dog that has wet the carpet and now slinks under the couch with his tail between his legs does not manifest conscience but something I would rather call anticipatory anxiety—more specifically, the fearful expectation of punishment—and this might well be the result of conditioning processes. It has nothing to do with conscience, because true conscience has nothing to do with the fearful expectation of punishment. As long as a man is still motived by either the fear of punishment or the hope of reward—or, for that matter, by the wish to appease the superego—conscience has not yet had its say.

Konrad Lorenz was cautious enough to speak of "moral*analoges* Verhalten bei Tieren" (behavior in animals that is *analogous* to moral behavior in man). By contrast, the reductionists do not recognize a qualitative difference between the two types of behavior. They deny that a uniquely human phenomenon exists at all. And they do so not on empirical grounds, as one might assume, but on the basis of an a priori denial. They insist that there is nothing in man which cannot be found in animals as well. Or, to vary a well-known dictum, *nihil est in homine, quod non prius fuerit in animalibus*. In this connection what comes to mind is the rabbi in the joke, who once was consulted by two parishioners. One man contended that the other's cat had stolen and eaten up five pounds of butter. The other contended that his cat did not care for butter. "Bring me the cat," the rabbi ordered. They brought him the cat. "Now bring me scales," he continued. And they brought him scales. "How many pounds of butter did you say the cat has eaten?" he asked. "Five pounds, Rabbi," was the answer. Thereupon the rabbi put the cat on the scales and, believe it or not, it weighed exactly five pounds. "Now I have the butter," the rabbi said, "but where is the cat?" He had started with the a priori assumption that if there are five pounds, it must be five pounds of butter. But is it not the same with the reductionists? They too start with the a priori assumption that if there is anything in man, it must be possible to explain it along the lines of animal behavior. Eventually they discover in man all the conditioned reflexes, conditioning processes, innate releasing mechanisms and whatever else they have been in search of. "Now we have it," they say, like the rabbi, "but where is—man?"

Conscience is a human phenomenon, I said before, and therefore must not be dealt with reductionistically—that is to say, on a subhuman level, be it in exclusively behavioristic terms or psychodynamic ones. Nor must a neurosis stemming from the repression of conscience be treated solely on the grounds of behavioristic or psychodynamic concepts. There is a publication, for instance, on a case of "existential depression"* that was treated by the behavior-therapeutic technique called "thought-stopping." The patient had been suffering from "negative thoughts about himself" due to "negative self-evaluation." Since his depression was considered an "existential" one, it is fair to assume that it was his conscience which caused the negative "responses to his own behavior" and even "repeated suicide attempts." From this it follows that treating the "negative thoughts by thought-stopping procedures" amounted to a repression of conscience, which Martin Heidegger taught us to regard as a wired-in existential monitor (the oversimplification is mine).

The following is a case in which psychoanalysis

* Zev W. Wanderer, "Existential Depression Treated by Desensitization of Phobias: Strategy and Transcript," *Journal of Behavior Therapy and Experimental Psychiatry*, 3 (1972), pp. 111–16.

rather than behavior modification induced the repression of conscience:

Since the Summer of 1973 I have been employed as an assistant psychologist by two psychiatrists in San Diego. During my supervision sessions I often disagreed with the psychoanalytic theory that my employers sought to teach me. Yet, as their manner was very authoritarian, I was fearful of expressing my contrary opinions. I feared that I might lose my job. I therefore suppressed my own opinions to a large degree. After several months of this self-suppression, I began to feel anxiety during my supervision sessions. I began to accept the therapeutic aid of some of my friends. However, we succeeded only in making the anxiety problem worse; for what did we do but approach the problem in a somewhat psychoanalytic manner? We sought to uncover the early traumas in me that were causing my transference anxiety with my supervisors. We studied my early relationship to my father, etc., to no avail. Thus, I increasingly found myself in a state of hyper-reflection, and my condition grew worse. My anxiety rose to such a level at my supervision sessions that I had to mention it to the psychiatrists in order to explain my behavior. They recommended that I see a psychoanalytically oriented psychotherapist for personal therapy in order to get to the hidden meaning of this anxiety. Not being able to afford such professional help, my friends and I increased our efforts to uncover the deep hidden meaning of my anxiety, and I became worse. I often had extreme anxiety attacks. My recovery began with Dr. Frankl's class, Man's Search for Meaning, on January 8, 1974. I heard Dr. Frankl speak of the difficulties encountered when one tries to psychoanalytically unmask an authentic response. During that four-hour class I began to see how the therapy I had undergone had increased my problem: an iatrogenic neurosis almost. I began to see that it was my own self-suppression in the supervision sessions that had caused my anxiety. My disagreement with the psychiatrists and my fear of expressing this disagreement had caused my reaction. I quickly ended the therapy and felt better upon doing so. Yet the real change came during my next supervision session. During this session I began to express my opinions and disagreements with the psychiatrists when I actually felt such disagreements. I felt no fear of losing my job, for my peace of mind had become far more important than my job. As I began to express myself in this session, I immediately felt my anxiety beginning to decrease. In the past two weeks, my anxiety has decreased by about 90 percent.

So conscience is a human phenomenon. However, it can be an all too human phenomenon. It not only leads us to meaning but may also lead us astray. This is part and parcel of the human condition. Conscience may err, and I cannot know absolutely for certain whether my conscience is right and another's conscience, which tells him something different, is wrong, or whether the reverse is true. Not that there is no truth: there is. And there can be only one truth. But no one can be absolutely sure it is he who has arrived at this truth.

So man can only stick to his conscience, although, until he lies on his deathbed, he never knows whether it is the true meaning his conscience mediates to him. As Gordon W. Allport so beautifully put it, "we can be at one and the same time half-sure and whole-hearted" ("Psychological Models for Guidance," *Harvard Educational Review,* 32 [1962], p. 373).

Meanings refer to unique situations—and the equally unique persons confronting them. In contrast to the meanings, which are unique, values are more or less universal in that they are shared by whole segments of a given population. I would even define values as meaning-universals. As such, however, they are subjected to changes, and even more, they are affected by the present decay of traditions. (This cultural climate, after all, is reflected and mirrored on the personal level by the feeling of meaninglessness, by the inner void, by what I have described and termed the existential vacuum.) Traditions and values are crumbling. But meanings are not—cannot be—transmitted by traditions because in contrast to values, which are universal, meanings are unique. And as such they are transmitted, mediated to one's consciousness, by personal conscience.

In an age such as ours, in the age of meaninglessness, education, instead of confining itself to transmitting traditions and knowledge, must see its principal assignment in refining the individual's conscience—his only capacity still to find meanings despite the wane of traditions and values. In other words, the crumbling of universal values can be counteracted only by finding the unique meanings. In an age in which the Ten Commandments are losing their unconditional validity in the eyes of many people, man must be equipped with the capacity to listen to and obey the ten thousand demands and commandments hidden in the ten thousand situations with which life is confronting him. And it is these demands that are revealed to him by an alert conscience. Only then, by virtue of an alert conscience, can he also resist the effects of the existential vacuum as intimated at the outset, namely, conformism and totalitarianism.

A doctor cannot give meanings to his patients. Nor can a professor give meanings to his students. What they may give, however, is an example, the existential example of personal commitment to the search for truth.* As a matter of fact, the answer to the question What is the meaning of life? can only be given out of one's whole being—one's life is itself the answer to the question of its meaning. In other words, morals have to be not only ontologized but also existentialized.

It is a tenet of logotherapy that the humanness of man is grounded in his sense of responsibility (cf. Viktor E. Frankl, *The Doctor and the Soul* [New York: Alfred A. Knopf, 1965]). Man is responsible for fulfilling the meaning of his life. Being human means responding to life situations, replying to the questions they ask. Being human means answering these calls—but who is calling? To whom is man responding? These questions cannot be answered by logotherapy. It is the patient who must answer them. Logotherapy can only heighten the patient's innate awareness of his responsibility, and this responsibility includes being responsible for one's answer to the question of how to interpret his life, that is to say, whether along the lines of theism or atheism.

From this it follows that logotherapy does not at all "hover close to authoritarianism," and least of all does it amount to "taking over the patient's responsibility and diminishing him as a person" (Rollo May, *Existential Psychology* [New York: Random House; second edition, 1969]). On the contrary, logotherapy can be defined as education to responsibility (Karl Dienelt, *Von Freud zu Frankl* [Vienna: Österreichischer Bundesverlag, 1967]).

* The professor's existential vacuum may be transmitted as well. "If teachers show in their attitudes and actions that they are cynical, bored and defeated, the young will get the message, no matter how many literary classics they are required to read." (Arthur G. Wirth, "Education as Meaning," in Reuven P. Bulka and Joseph B. Fabry, eds., *Aspects of Logotherapy* [in preparation].)

However, I would say that at present responsibility must be defined as selectivity. We are living in an affluent society, and this is an affluence not only of material goods but of various sorts of stimuli as well. We are bombarded by the mass media. We are bombarded by sexual stimuli. And, last but not least, the information explosion represents a further, new affluence. Heaps of books and journals pile up on our desks. Unless we wish to drown in total (not only sexual) promiscuity, we have to choose between what is important and what is not, what is meaningful and what is not. We have to become selective and discriminating.

When addressing the 1967 Conference of College Presidents, which was sponsored by the Institute of Higher Education of Teachers College, Columbia University, I concluded by saying, "I venture to predict here and now the surge of a new sense of responsibleness."* The rise of this responsibleness was noticeable particularly among the youth. I saw its first signs in the protest movements, although I frankly had to confess that much of this protesting was better described as anti-testing because it was struggling not for something but, rather, against something. But this is quite understandable because the young people are caught in the existential vacuum. They do not know anything worthy of being fought for, and there are so many things to be against. However, I am sure that sooner or later they will come up with positive, constructive, creative alternatives. This should not be difficult. After all, many tasks are in store for them, waiting to be completed by them. They have only to widen their hori-

* Note also a statement in the documents of Vatican II: "We are witnesses of the birth of a new humanism, one in which man is defined first of all by his responsibility."

zons and to notice that there is much meaning to be fulfilled around them.

This would entail and engender a sense of co-respon-
sibility. I remember that in Canada students were fasting,
and citizens were invited to pay a certain amount for
each hour that a student went without food. The students
sent the money to Biafra. At the same time we had a lot
of snow in Vienna, and there was a labor shortage because so few people cared to do the menial work of shovel-
ing snow. Students from the University of Vienna volun-
teered to do the job and sent that money to Biafra, too.
Here I see examples of a growing concern with other people on a planetary level, an increasing sense of worldwide
solidarity.

The emphasis that logotherapy places on responsibility not only effectuates in the patient a growing awareness of his own responsibility, but also precludes moralizing on the part of the therapist. Logotherapy is neither
teaching nor preaching. The logotherapist does not "sup-
ply the patient with his goal" (Rollo May, *Existential
Psychology*). If he ever did, he was no logotherapist.
After all, it was not a logotherapist but a psychoanalyst
whom F. Gordon Pleune described as "a moralist first and
foremost" ("All Dis-Ease Is Not Disease," *International
Journal of Psycho-Analysis*, 46 [1965], p. 358). And it
was not logotherapy but psychoanalysis that was defined
by E. Mansell Pattison as "a moral enterprise whose central concern is morality" ("Ego morality," *Psychoanalytic
Review*, 55 [1968], pp. 187–222). The logotherapist
leaves it to the patient to decide what is meaningful and
what is not, or, for that matter, what is good and what is
bad. This abstinence from value judgments, however, is
not a universally accepted principle. To quote, for a

change, representatives of behavior therapy, L. Krasner states that "it is the therapist who is making decisions as to what is good and bad behavior" (quoted in David Grossman, "Of Whose Unscientific Methods and Unaware Values?" *Psychotherapy*, 5 [1968], p. 53). Joseph Wolpe and Arnold A. Lazarus even "do not shrink from attacking on rational grounds a patient's religious beliefs if they are a source of suffering" (*Behavior Therapy Techniques*, [Oxford, England: Pergamon Press, 1966]).

The fact remains that a psychiatrist cannot show the patient what, in a given situation, the meaning is. But he may well show the patient that there is a meaning and, as we shall see, that life not only holds a meaning, a unique meaning, for each and every man, but also never ceases to hold such a meaning—that it retains it, that it remains meaningful literally up to its last moment, to one's last breath. The patient then will see a meaning in his life under any conditions. In a word, he will become, and be, aware that the meaning of life is an unconditional one.

What we here embark on is not the value judgment of facts but rather factual statements about values. What we are engaged in is the phenomenological analysis of the valuing process as it goes on in the man in the street (who has not been exposed to *reductionist indoctrination*, be it on American campuses or analytical couches) whenever he sets out to find the meaning of his life. And the unbiased man in the street, indeed, does not understand himself as a battleground for the clashing claims of ego, id and superego. Nor does he see himself as the pawn and plaything of conditioning processes or drives and instincts. By virtue of what I call the *pre-reflective ontological self-understanding*, or what is called "the wisdom of the heart," he knows that being human means being responsible for fulfilling the meaning potential inherent in a given life situation. What is even more important, the man in the street knows that meaning may not only be found in creating a work and doing a deed, not only in encountering someone and experiencing something, but also, if need be, in the way in which he stands up to suffering.

As we see, the unbiased analysis of the unbiased man in the street reveals how he actually experiences values. Such an analysis is phenomenological, and as such it refrains from any preconceived patterns of interpretation and abstains from forcing phenomena into the Procrustean bed of pet concepts along the lines of a particular indoctrination, pet concepts such as "underlying psychodynamics" or "operant conditioning."

The phenomenological analysis of the man in the street yields those immediate data of experience from which, eventually, an entire axiology may be derived. Specifically, three chief groups of values may be discerned. I have classified them in terms of "creative, experiential and attitudinal values" (*The Doctor and the Soul*). As a matter of fact, it is only on the basis of this axiological trichotomy that life's unconditional meaningfulness can be maintained. It is through attitudinal values that even the negative, tragic aspects of human existence, or what I call the "tragic triad"—pain, guilt and death—may be turned into something positive and creative. Caught in a hopeless situation as its helpless victim, facing a fate that cannot be changed, man still may turn his predicament into an achievement and accomplishment at the human level. He thus may bear witness to the human potential at its best, which is to turn tragedy into triumph. "The measure of a man is the way he bears up under misfortune," as Plutarch once put it.

Logotherapy is, as it were, trifocal: it focuses on three fundamental facts of human existence: there is a will to meaning; there is a meaning in suffering; and there is a freedom of will. As to the last, man's freedom of choice concerns the freedom to choose not only one's own way of living, but even of dying.

The logotherapeutic emphasis on the potential meaning of unavoidable suffering has nothing to do with masochism. Masochism means accepting unnecessary suffering; but I explicitly referred to "a fate that cannot be changed." What can be changed should be changed. Let me illustrate this by an advertisement which was couched in the following verse:

> Calmly bear, without ado,
> That which fate imposed on you;
> But to bedbugs don't resign:
> Turn for help to Rosenstein (644 W. 161 St.)!

The phenomenological analysis of the wisdom of the heart of the man in the street discloses that he is cognizant of creative, experiential and attitudinal values. Further, he knows that attitudinal values rank higher than creative and experiential values. In other words, he also is cognizant of their hierarchy. It goes to the credit of Elisabeth S. Lukas to have offered statistical evidence that the man in the street is fully aware of both the trichotomy of values and their hierarchy. Dr. Lukas based her research on computerized data obtained from 1,340 subjects.

Empirical corroboration and confirmation that life is unconditionally meaningful was contributed by some of the several dozens of research projects that have been based on the PIL Test developed by James C. Crumbaugh. There is, for example, a study with 40 Air Force servicemen and 40 hospitalized male schizophrenics. It "showed that scores on the Purpose-in-Life Test are not related to age or IQ." (Thomas D. Yarnell, "Purpose-in-Life Test: Further Correlates," *Journal of Individual Psychology*, 27 [1971], pp. 76–79.) "This would fit Crumbaugh's finding of no correlation between PIL scores and educational level. It appears then that life can be considered meaningful regardless of age, IQ, or educational level." For the meaning of life is unconditional ultimately with respect to outer as well as inner conditions. An interesting result of the research conducted and reported by S. Kratochvil and I. Planova of the Department of Psychology, University of Brno, Czechoslovakia, reported by the authors at an international congress, reads: "Unfavorable circumstances in life may but do not have to frustrate one existentially; it depends on one's value system"—i.e., it is dependent on whether or not one is aware of attitudinal values as a meaning potential to fulfill, if need be. As to inner conditions, Jann Ruch has shown that "individuals with a wide variety of personality traits may experience meaning in life." On the other hand, "no personality trait insures against an existential vacuum." (Paper presented to the Logotherapy Institute at the United States International University, San Diego, 1973.) In another study, authored by Joseph A. Durlak of Vanderbilt University, "a significant negative correlation was found between purpose in life and fear of death ($r = -.68$, $p < .001$). Results thus supported Frankl's notions that Ss who reported a high purpose and meaning in their life tended to fear death less and to have a more accepting attitude toward it. In comparison, Ss who reported less purpose and meaning in their life showed a higher fear of death." ("Relationship between Individual Attitudes toward Life and Death," *Journal of Consulting and Clinical Psychology*, 38 [1972], p. 463.) In this context, however, it seems to be most important to hear from the author that the recognition of the unconditional meaningfulness of life is not even dependent on our being religious or irreligious. "It does not appear," he says, "that a belief in a God and in a future existence after death could serve as an explanation for the different attitudes toward life and death found."

This is perfectly in accordance with Augustine Meier's findings. His research study ("Frankl's 'Will to Meaning' as Measured by the Purpose-in-Life Test in Relation to Age and Sex Differences," dissertation, University of Ottawa, 1973) "indicates that the educational background and the religious affiliation of the subjects are not related to variations in the mean scores on the PIL." Leonard Murphy ("Extent of Purpose-in-Life and Four Frankl-proposed Life Objectives," dissertation, University of Ottawa, 1967) already had "found evidence to show that people who had chosen God and [those who chose] another person as their life objective did not differ significantly in their scores on the PIL. Both groups found equal meaning for their lives." In Meier's study, however, subjects were taken from five different religious denominations, and it is his contention that "the inability to find evidence to show that subjects differ on the PIL scores on the basis of religious differences gives support to Frankl's idea that God, as experienced by different religious affiliations, can give equal meaning to subjects." In addition, Meier found evidence to show that "sex and PIL are not related variables." The evidence of his study, Meier believes, "supports Frankl's idea that all people are equally capable of finding similar intensities of meaning." More specifically, evidence from Meier's study shows that "the 13–15 age group has access to experiential values in particular, the 45–55 age group appears to derive 'meaning in life' from the actualization and discovery of creative values, the 65 and over age group derives its meaning from the discovery and actualization of attitudinal values."

We psychiatrists are neither teachers nor preachers but have to learn from the man in the street, from his pre-reflective ontological self-understanding, what being human is all about. We have to learn from his *sapientia cordis*, from the wisdom of his heart, that being human means being confronted continually with situations, each of which is at once a chance and a challenge, giving us a "chance" to fulfill ourselves by meeting the "challenge" to fulfill its meaning. Each situation is a call, first to listen, and then to respond.

As I see it, it is the assignment of phenomenology to translate this wisdom of the heart into scientific terms. If morals are to survive they must not only be ontologized and existentialized, but also phenomenologized. Thus the man in the street becomes the true teacher of morals.

Let me illustrate by quoting from a write-up on the seminars at the University of Chicago's Billings Hospital: "Unseen behind a one-way glass, medical students, social workers, nurses and aides, chaplains and student chaplains watch sufferers from illnesses which most often are fatal come to an understanding with death. In an entirely real sense, *the patients are teachers*—through their own experience—about the end of life." (*Time* Magazine, February 2, 1968, pp. 38–40.)

A sense of fulfillment is available to the man in the street, indeed, in the face of dying—and suffering. To demonstrate this let me again take up the letter mentioned in the Preface, received from a prisoner at the Baltimore County Prison. There was a man who was "financially ruined, in jail," and yet "at complete peace" with himself and the world after he had found a meaning in even such a miserable life. He concluded the letter by exclaiming, "how wonderful life is. I embrace today, anxiously await tomorrow."

The pre-reflective ontological self-understanding really consists of two aspects: "a prelogical understanding of being" and "a premoral understanding of meaning" (see p. 33). In some cases, however, both aspects are repressed. Neither is compatible with indoctrination along the lines of a reductionist philosophy of life. This results in nihilism, against which a reaction formation is then built up, namely, cynicism. I once had to take over the treatment of an outstanding psychoanalyst who was caught in a severe depression resulting from nihilism. It was hard to help him find his way to the existential ground on which the direction and vision of values again were available to him—available to him because he *was himself* the direction and vision. There is a point at which being and meaning merge. This, after all, is the reason why the premoral understanding of meaning is rooted in the prelogical understanding of being, and both are blended into the pre-reflective ontological self-understanding.

Even in diehard positivists the wisdom of the heart

may supersede the knowledge of the brain and allow for recognizing the unconditional meaningfulness of life through the potential meaning of suffering. From this I would not even exempt the nihilists. "It is strange," a graduate psychology student of the University of California at Berkeley writes in a letter to me: "The nihilists first laugh at your concept of meaning through suffering —and ultimately their tears dissolve them."

It is obvious that Nicholas Mosley was right when he wrote that "there is a subject nowadays which is taboo in the way that sexuality was once taboo, which is to talk about life as if it had any meaning." (*Natalie, Natalia* [New York: Popular Library, 1972].) It therefore is understandable that logotherapy is facing some resistance. It is no longer confronted, and concerned, with instinctual and sexual frustrations and repressions but with the frustration—and consequent repression—of the will to meaning. Not *eros* but *logos* is the victim of repression. Once the will to meaning is repressed, however, the existence of meaning is no longer perceived.

Logotherapy aims to unlock the will to meaning and to assist the patient in seeing a meaning in his life. In so doing, however, it leans on the phenomenological analysis of the pre-reflective ontological self-understanding. It borrows from what the patient knows by virtue of the wisdom of his heart, at the bottom of his heart, in the depth of his unconscious. This knowledge is brought to the surface of consciousness. And if it has been my contention that *phenomenology* means *translating* the wisdom of the heart into scientific terms, I now may add another definition: *logotherapy* means *retranslating* this wisdom of the heart into plain words, into the language of the man in the street so that he may benefit from it. And it *is* possible to convey it to him. Let me just recall what happened when I spoke to the prisoners of San Quentin in 1966, at the request of the prison's director. After I had addressed these prisoners, who were the toughest criminals in California, one stood up and said, "Dr. Frankl, would you be kind enough to say a few words through the mike to Aaron Mitchell, who is expecting his death in the gas chamber in a couple of days? The people from Death Row are not allowed to come down to the Chapel, but perhaps you will say a few words particularly to him." (An embarrassing position; but I had to take this challenge and say a few words.) I improvisingly said, "Mr. Mitchell, believe me, I understand your situation. I myself had to live for some time in the shadow of a gas chamber. But also believe me that even then I did not give up my conviction of the unconditional meaningfulness of life, because either life has a meaning—and then it must retain this meaning even if it is shortly lived—or life has no meaning—and then just adding ever more years and perpetuating this meaningless job could not be of any meaning either. And believe me, even a life that has been meaningless all along, that is, a life that has been wasted, may—even in the last moment—still be bestowed with meaning by the very way in which we tackle this situation." And I told him the story that is laid down in Leo Tolstoy's novel *The Death of Ivan Ilyich* —the tale of a man who is about sixty years of age and suddenly learns that he is to die in a couple of days. But by the insight he gains, not only in this fact but also in the very fact that he has wasted his life, that his life has been virtually meaningless—by this insight he rises above himself, he grows beyond himself and thereby finally becomes capable—retroactively—of flooding his life with infinite meaning.

To all appearances, this message got across. If I had doubted it, I would have been convinced later, when I came across, in the May 10 *San Francisco Chronicle,* a report on an "unusual press conference" that Aaron Mitchell "began by handing out this brief statement he had typed himself: 'I have made my appeal to God and to the Governor. This is my last appeal to Man. Forgive me, for I knew not.' As he met newspaper reporters at the prison under the careful eyes of guards, Mitchell said, 'I don't really expect clemency from the Governor and I sympathize with him. He will be under criticism either way, but much lighter criticism if he fails to act for me.' The condemned man, seemingly much calmer than his interviewers, also said he feared his own execution may start 'a long new line to the gas chamber.' Mitchell acknowledged the drizzle of rain outside: 'It always seems to rain when things are bad, and the rain is God in anger.' The first friends he ever had in his life, he said, were two Death Row guards who appeared at his sentence-determining penalty trial after he had been waiting in the prison. 'It was the first time in my entire life someone was willing to stand up and say I know this man, I'll speak in his behalf,' Mitchell told reporters. 'What I'd like to feel, these last days I have of life, is that if you're home, or in the office, at work or play when you read this, stand up and say to yourself, I feel as if I know this man. He could have been my friend. Because I feel the need of friends in my dying hour,' he said."

We must not overlook and forget that even self-administered logotherapy may be helpful, and may even change the life of professionals. In this context, I would like to quote from two letters I recently received.

> All of my life I have been in engineering management. I am presently in a salary bracket which puts me in the upper 2 percent of salaries earned in the United States. Yet in spite of my relatively high salary and the responsible positions I have held I felt an emptiness in my life. It has only been in the last few years that my life started to have meaning. Logotherapy clearly put my life in perspective and allowed me to gain an understanding which I had never had before. I am now in the process of changing my profession from engineering management to clinical psychology. I will not make as much money or be in as responsible a position as I am now in, but I know that the direction I have taken will have more meaning for me regardless of money or position.

Here the frustrated will to meaning had been compensated by the will to power ("position") plus what one might call a "will to money." The man had belonged with those who have the means—the financial means—but no meaning. However, once his will to meaning had been reawakened and meaning began to dawn upon him, any overconcern with money (which is the mere means to an end rather than the end itself) subsided. And here is the second letter:

> As a therapist I was primarily Freudian by training. All that Freudian philosophy had promised, I had received in abundance—sixty-thousand-dollar home with pool, two late-model cars, three healthy, bright children, loving wife and companion and an occupation that brought pride and accept-

ance from the community—but still something was missing. I felt the existential vacuum. I had accepted the tranquil state as being the end result of therapy. Now that I have reestablished a new quest in my life, the existential vacuum is dissipating. I face surgery of the esophagus and stomach within the next two months. Instead of depression I find myself facing this with the feeling that the experience will make me a better person. The forced loss of thirty-five pounds will certainly be part of this.

Here, as we see, the rediscovery of meaning even included attitudinal values.

That meaning can be found not only in spite of, but also because of unavoidable suffering, such as an incurable disease—say, an inoperable cancer—is a possibility more easily understood by the man in the street than by the expert in the field. Beverly Hills realtor Fred Harris had inoperable cancer of both lungs. According to a report published in *Time* Magazine for August 14, 1972, he formed a self-help program through which cancer victims who have more or less adjusted to their illness counsel others who have not. Judd Marmor rightly commented that the project "can also be therapeutic for the person who is doing the helping. It gives him a purpose in life at a point where the curtain seems to be drawing down."

Other authors, however, are not prepared to take such a motivation at its face value. In *Life-Threatening Behavior*, the official journal of the American Association of Suicidology, Paul H. Blachly of the University of Oregon Medical School once suggested that the suicidal person who wants to destroy his whole body may find an alternative in sacrificing just a part of it, by donating either blood or an organ to a person who needs it to live. One would assume that Blachly advocates an approach similar to

logotherapy, which teaches that suicide may be caused
by a feeling of meaninglessness and that its prevention
accordingly presupposes that the patient discover a meaning to life. However, this is not so. Blachly apparently
does not see man as a being in search of meaning. He
therefore cannot understand either that man is willing to
sacrifice everything if there is meaning in such a sacrifice,
or, the corollary of this proposition, that man does not
care for a life without meaning. Once we eliminate from
our vision of man the human dimension in which such
human phenomena as the will to meaning are located, we
must construct, not to say invent, drives and instincts in
order to explain "human" behavior—without recognizing
that by the very nature of such an explanation man's behavior actually is dehumanized. Small wonder that
Blachly is compelled to hypothesize a "death wish," and
believes that a patient who is prone to suicide is a plaything of the death wish. To be sure, this wish "might be
purged if the donor gives an organ that is not essential
to his own life. People who donate a kidney," Blachly
notes, "often experience a sustained feeling of satisfaction"—satisfaction of the death wish, that is. In actual
fact, I would say, these people have discovered a meaning
to life and a reason for survival. However, a psychology
that a priori shuts out meaning and reason of course cannot recognize the self-transcendent quality of the human
reality and instead must resort to drives and instincts.
Whenever the pulling force exerted by meanings and reasons is scotomized, the pushing force of drives and instincts is hypothesized.*

---

* If self-transcendence is denied and the door to meanings and values is
closed, reasons and motives are replaced by conditioning processes. This
opens the door to manipulation, and it is up to the "hidden persuaders"

Before, I spoke of meaningful suffering in terms of sacrifice; in this context a story comes to mind that, because of its brevity, I like to tell my students in order to illustrate how suffering may be bestowed with meaning. It is the story of a physician who suffered from a severe depression after his wife died. I embarked on a short Socratic dialogue by asking him what would have happened if he had died first. "How much she would have suffered," he answered. What was now left to me was simply to respond, "Your wife has been spared this suffering, and after all, it is you who are sparing her this suffering—to be sure, at the price that now you have to survive and mourn her." At the same moment, he could see a meaning in his suffering, the meaning of a sacrifice. There was still suffering, but no longer despair. Because *despair is suffering without meaning*.

When I tell this brief story I am often blamed for having "imposed" meanings and values on the patient. As it happens, however, it can be shown that what I actually did was intuitively to elicit from the patient what "the man in the street" knows by virtue of the "wisdom of the heart." Edwin S. Shneidman provided clear-cut

---

to do the conditioning, to manipulate man. And vice versa. If one is to manipulate human beings he has to indoctrinate them along the lines of pan-determinism. "Only by dispossessing autonomous man," says B. F. Skinner, "can we turn to the real causes of human behavior—from the inaccessible to the manipulable." (*Beyond Freedom and Dignity* [New York: Alfred A. Knopf, 1971].) I quite simply think, first of all, that conditioning processes are not the real causes of human behavior; secondly, that its real cause is something accessible, provided that the humanness of human behavior is not denied on a priori grounds; and, thirdly, that the humanness of human behavior cannot be revealed unless we recognize that the real "cause" of a given individual's behavior is not a cause but, rather, a reason. What, then, is the difference between causes and reasons? If you cut onions you weep. Your tears have a cause. But you have no reason to weep. . . .

"empirical data" relevant to the issue at hand. He distributed to the students at Harvard a class questionnaire that included the question "If and when you are married, would you prefer to outlive your spouse or would you prefer your spouse to outlive you?" The typical male response was in fact to choose to die after his wife.

As an interlude, let us imagine what help could have been offered to the physician whose wife had died if a rigidly orthodox behavior therapist had had to tackle the situation. Let us see what behavior modifiers suggest "when death or some other irrevocable happening deprives one of something cherished. . . . A schedule should be devised by which the individual's efforts are systematically rewarded, sometimes starting with such minor accomplishments as making a telephone call, mowing the lawn, or washing dishes. These behaviors are praised and in other ways rewarded by the therapist, and after a time come to give the patient a sense of satisfaction quite directly." (Joseph Wolpe, "Neurotic Depression," *American Journal of Psychotherapy*, 25 [1971], pp. 362–68.) Let us hope.

As to the feeling of meaninglessness, per se, it is an existential despair and a spiritual distress rather than an emotional disease or a mental illness. This, however, in no way implies that we must discard and abolish the medical model. What we must do is simply recognize its limits. Within these limits, mental illness is no "myth" at all, but we have to distinguish among the various levels at which its etiological point of departure may be located. Mental illness may be psychogenic (neurosis) or somatogenic (psychosis) in nature and origin. But noögenic and (psych-) iatrogenic (pseudo-) neuroses also exist.

And, last but not least, the existential vacuum exists. It is something sociogenic and not at all a neurosis.

It is important that this be conveyed to the "non-patients" suffering from it. They should know that despair over the apparent meaninglessness of life constitutes a human achievement rather than a neurosis. After all, no animal cares whether or not its existence has a meaning. It is the prerogative of man to quest for a meaning to his life, and also to question whether such a meaning exists. This is a manifestation of intellectual sincerity and honesty. In particular, it is a privilege of youth not to take for granted that there is a fixed meaning to life, but boldly to dare to challenge it. However, this courage should be matched by patience. People should be patient enough to wait until, sooner or later, meaning dawns upon them. This is what they should do. Rather than taking their lives —or taking refuge in drugs.

All this should be conveyed to man by way of "first aid" in cases of existential vacuum. To demonstrate how important such first aid might be, I would like to quote Albert Einstein: "The man who regards his life as meaningless is not merely unhappy but hardly fit for life." Indeed, survival is dependent on direction. However, survival cannot be the supreme value. Unless life points to something beyond itself, survival is pointless and meaningless. It is not even possible. This is the very lesson I learned in three years spent in Auschwitz and Dachau, and in the meantime it has been confirmed by psychiatrists in prisoner-of-war camps: Only those who were oriented toward the future, toward a goal in the future, toward a meaning to fulfill in the future, were likely to survive.

And I think that this is not only true for the survival

of individuals but also holds for the survival of mankind. For there is hope for mankind's survival only as long as or as soon as people will arrive at the awareness of common denominators in axiological terms—that is to say, common denominators in what they feel makes their lives worth living. It is thus obvious that the subject boils down to an axiological issue: Will there be values and meanings that can be shared by people—and peoples? Values and meanings they might have in common?

The only thing I know for sure is that if common values and meanings are to be found, another step must be taken, a step now, thousands of years after mankind developed monotheism, the belief in the one God. Monotheism is not enough; it will not do. What we need is not only the belief in the one God but also the awareness of the one mankind, the awareness of the unity of humanity. I would call it *mon-anthropism*.

There is survival value in the will to meaning, as we have seen; but as to mankind, there is hope for survival only if mankind is united by a *common* will to a *common* meaning—in other words, by an awareness of common tasks. In the paper quoted previously, Carolyn Wood Sherif reported the results of experiments with children in whom group aggressions had been built up. However, once they were united by the common task of dragging a carriage out of the mud, the kids "forgot" to live out their group aggressions. Let us learn the lesson.

Yet we psychiatrists should refrain from dabbling in fields other than our own. I would say that each issue deserves to be taken up by a specialist. So why not leave something, say, to the sociologists? We psychiatrists simply don't have the answer for each and every question. Least of all do we have a prescription to hand out when it comes to the question of how to cure all the ills and ailments that afflict our society. *Let us start humanizing psychiatry—rather than divinizing it*—and, to begin with, let us stop ascribing divine attributes to psychiatrists. We psychiatrists are neither omniscient nor omnipotent —we are only omnipresent: we are present at all symposia, and mingling in all discussions. . . .

As to logotherapy, it is not a panacea.* It therefore is open to cooperation with other approaches to psychotherapy; it is open to its own evolution; and it is open to religion. This is indispensable. It is true, logotherapy deals with the *logos*; it deals with meaning. Specifically, I see the meaning of logotherapy in helping others to see meaning in life. But one cannot "give" meaning to the life of others. And if this is true of meaning per se, how much more does it hold for ultimate meaning. *The more comprehensive the meaning, the less comprehensible it is.* Infinite meaning is necessarily beyond the comprehension of a finite being. Here is the point at which science gives up and wisdom takes over. "Consider a poor dog whom they are vivisecting in a laboratory," William James said when addressing the Harvard Young Men's Christian Association. "He cannot see a single redeeming ray in the whole business; and yet all these diabolic-seeming events are often controlled by human intentions with which, if his poor benighted mind could only be made to catch a glimpse of them, all that is heroic in him would religiously

---

* The statement that logotherapy is not a panacea—as much as it might disarm its adversaries—may disappoint its admirers. Edgar Krout of West Georgia College confronted its students with a number of statements quoted from the literature in the field of logotherapy. While there was about 90 percent general agreement with them, some 50 percent of the students were reluctant to credit one of the statements: they did not want to accept the fact that logotherapy is no panacea.

acquiesce. Lying on his back on the board there he may be performing a function incalculably higher than any that prosperous canine life admits of; and yet, of the whole performance, this function is the one portion that must remain absolutely beyond his ken. Now turn from this to the life of man. Although we only see our world, and the dog's within it, yet encompassing both these worlds a still wider world may be there, as unseen by us as our world is by him."*

Wisdom is knowledge plus: knowledge—and the knowledge of its own limits.

* William James, *The Will to Believe* (New York: Longmans, 1897).

English Bibliography
of Logotherapy and Existenzanalyse

1. BOOKS

Bulka, Reuven P., and Joseph B. Fabry, eds., *Aspects of Logotherapy* (in preparation).
Crumbaugh, James C., *Everything to Gain: A Guide to Self-fulfillment Through Logoanalysis.* Chicago, Nelson-Hall, 1973.
Fabry, Joseph B., *The Pursuit of Meaning: Logotherapy Applied to Life.* Preface by Viktor E. Frankl. Boston, Beacon Press, 1968; paperback edition, *A Guide to the Theory and Application of Viktor E. Frankl's Logotherapy,* 1969.
Frankl, Viktor E., *Man's Search for Meaning: An Introduction to Logotherapy.* Preface by Gordon W. Allport. Boston, Beacon Press, 1959; paperback edition, New York, Touchstone, 1973.
——, *The Doctor and the Soul: From Psychotherapy to Logotherapy.* New York, Alfred A. Knopf, Inc.; second, expanded edition, 1965; paperback edition, New York, Vintage Books, 1973.
——, *Psychotherapy and Existentialism: Selected Papers on Logotherapy.* New York, Washington Square Press, 1967; Touchstone paperback, 1968.
——, *The Will to Meaning: Foundations and Applications of Logotherapy.* New York and Cleveland, The World Publishing Company, 1969; paperback edition, New York, New American Library, 1970.
Leslie, Robert C., *Jesus and Logotherapy: The Ministry of Jesus as*

Interpreted Through the Psychotherapy of Viktor Frankl. New York and Nashville, Abingdon Press, 1965; paperback edition, 1968.

Tweedie, Donald F., *Logotherapy and the Christian Faith: An Evaluation of Frankl's Existential Approach to Psychotherapy.* Preface by Viktor E. Frankl. Grand Rapids, Michigan, Baker Book House, 1961; paperback edition, 1965.

————, *The Christian and the Couch: An Introduction to Christian Logotherapy.* Grand Rapids, Mich., Baker Book House, 1963.

Ungersma, Aaron J., *The Search for Meaning: A New Approach in Psychotherapy and Pastoral Psychology.* Philadelphia, Westminster Press, 1961; paperback edition, Foreword by Viktor E. Frankl, 1968.

2. CHAPTERS IN BOOKS

Arnold, Magda B., and John A. Gasson, "Logotherapy and Existential Analysis," in *The Human Person.* New York, Ronald Press, 1954.

Barnitz, Harry W., "Frankl's Logotherapy," in *Existentialism and The New Christianity.* New York, Philosophical Library, 1969.

Elmore, Thomas M., and Eugene D. Chambres, "Anomie, Existential Neurosis and Personality: Relevance for Counseling," in *Proceedings,* 75th Annual Convention, American Psychological Association, 1967, 341–42.

Frankl, Viktor E., contributions to *Critical Incidents in Psychotherapy,* S. W. Standal and R. J. Corsini, eds. Englewood Cliffs, New Jersey, Prentice-Hall, 1959.

————, "Logotherapy and the Collective Neuroses," in *Progress in Psychotherapy,* J. H. Masserman and J. L. Moreno, eds. New York, Grune & Stratton, 1959.

————, "The Philosophical Foundations of Logotherapy" (paper read before the first Lexington Conference on Phenomenology on April 4, 1963), in *Phenomenology: Pure and Applied,* Erwin Straus, ed. Pittsburgh, Duquesne University Press, 1964.

————, "Fragments from the Logotherapeutic Treatment of Four Cases. With an Introduction and Epilogue by G. Kaczanowski," in *Modern Psychotherapeutic Practice: Innovations in Technique,* Arthur Burton, ed. Palo Alto, California, Science and Behavior Books, 1965.

————, "The Will to Meaning," in *Are You Nobody?* Richmond, Virginia, John Knox Press, 1966.

——, "Comment on Vatican II's Pastoral Constitution on the Church in the Modern World," in *World*. Chicago, Catholic Action Federations, 1967.

——, "Paradoxical Intention: A Logotherapeutic Technique," in *Active Psychotherapy*, Harold Greenwald, ed. New York, Atherton Press, 1967.

——, "The Significance of Meaning for Health," in *Religion and Medicine: Essays on Meaning, Values and Health*, David Belgum, ed. Ames, Iowa, The Iowa State University Press, 1967.

——, "Accepting Responsibility" and "Overcoming Circumstances," in *Man's Search for a Meaningful Faith: Selected Readings*, Judith Weidmann, ed. Nashville, Graded Press, 1967.

——, "The Task of Education in an Age of Meaninglessness," in *New Prospects for the Small Liberal Arts College*, Sidney S. Letter, ed. New York, Teachers College Press, 1968.

——, "Self-Transcendence as a Human Phenomenon," in *Readings in Humanistic Psychology*, Anthony J. Sutich and Miles A. Vich, eds. New York, The Free Press, 1969.

——, "Reductionism and Nihilism," in *Beyond Reductionism: New Perspectives in the Life Sciences* (The Alpbach Symposium, 1968), Arthur Koestler and J. R. Smythies, eds. New York, Macmillan, 1970.

——, "What is Meant by Meaning?" in *Values in an Age of Confrontation*, Jeremiah W. Canning, ed. Columbus, Ohio, Charles E. Merrill Publishing Company, 1970.

——, "Beyond Self-Actualization and Self-Expression," in *Perspectives on the Group Process: A Foundation for Counseling with Groups*, C. Gratton Kemp, ed. Boston, Houghton Mifflin Company, 1970.

——, "Logotherapy," in *Psychopathology Today: Experimentation, Theory and Research*, William S. Sahakian, ed. Itasca, Illinois, F. E. Peacock Publishers, 1970.

——, "Universities and the Quest for Peace," in *Report of the First World Conference on the Role of the University in the Quest for Peace*. Binghamton, N.Y., State University of New York, 1970.

——, "Youth in Search of Meaning," in *Students Search for Meaning*, James Edward Doty, ed. Kansas City, Missouri, The Lowell Press, 1971.

——, "Dynamics, Existence and Values" and "The Concept of Man in Logotherapy," in *Personality Theory: A Source Book*, Harold J. Vetter and Barry D. Smith, eds. New York, Appleton-Century-Crofts, 1971.

————, "Meaninglessness: A Challenge to Psychologists," in *Theories of Psychopathology and Personality*, Theodore Millon, ed. Philadelphia, W. B. Saunders Company, 1973.

————, "Beyond Pluralism and Determinism," in *Unity Through Diversity: A Festschrift for Ludwig von Bertalanffy*, William Ray and Nicholas D. Rizzo, eds. New York, Gordon and Breach, 1973.

————, "Encounter: The Concept and Its Vulgarization," in *Psychotherapy and Behavior Change 1973*, Hans H. Strupp et al., eds. Chicago, Aldine Publishing Company, 1974.

————, "Paradoxical Intention and Dereflection: Two Logotherapeutic Techniques," in *New Dimensions in Psychiatry: A World View*, Silvano Arieti, ed. New York, John Wiley & Sons, Inc., 1975.

Freilicher, M., "Applied Existential Psychology: Victor Frankl and Logotherapy," in *PsychoSources*, Evelyn Shapiro, ed. New York, Bantam Books, 1973.

Friedman, Maurice, "Viktor Frankl," in *The Worlds of Existentialism*. New York, Random House, 1964.

Howland, Elihu S., "Viktor Frankl," in *Speak Through the Earthquake: Religious Faith and Emotional Health*. Philadelphia, United Church Press, 1972.

Ledermann, E. K., "Viktor E. Frankl's Ontological Value Ethics," in *Existential Neurosis*. London, Butterworths, 1972.

Leslie, Robert, "Frankl's New Concept of Man," in *Contemporary Religious Issues*, Donald E. Hartsock, ed. Belmont, California, Wadsworth Publishing Company, 1968.

Liston, Robert A., "Viktor Frankl," in *Healing the Mind: Eight Views of Human Nature*. New York, Praeger, 1974.

Marks, Isaac M., "Paradoxical Intention ('Logotherapy')," in *Fears and Phobias*. New York, Academic Press, 1969.

————, "Paradoxical Intention," in *Behavior Modification*, W. Stewart Agras, ed. Boston, Little, Brown and Company, 1972.

Maslow, Abraham H., "Comments on Dr. Frankl's Paper," in *Readings in Humanistic Psychology*, Anthony J. Sutich and Miles A. Vich, eds. New York, The Free Press, 1969.

McKinney, Fred, "Man's Search for Meaning," in *Psychology in Action*. New York, Macmillan, 1967.

Misiak, Henry, and Virginia Staudt Sexton, "Logotherapy," in *Phenomenological, Existential, and Humanistic Psychologies: A Historical Survey*. New York, Grune & Stratton, 1973.

Patterson, C. H., "Frankl's Logotherapy," in *Theories of Counseling and Psychotherapy*. New York, Harper & Row, 1966.

Sahakian, William S., "Viktor Frankl," in *History of Psychology*. Itasca, Illinois; F. E. Peacock Publishers, Inc., 1968.

――, "Logotherapy," in *Psychotherapy and Counseling: Studies in Technique*. Chicago, Rand McNally, 1969.

――, "Logotherapy Approach to Personality," in *Psychology of Personality*. Chicago, Rand McNally, 1974.

Salit, Norman, "Existential Analysis; Logotherapy—the Gulf Narrows," in *The Worlds of Norman Salit*, Abraham Burstein, ed. New York, Bloch, 1966.

Schneider, Marius G., "The Existentialistic Concept of the Human Person in Viktor E. Frankl's Logotherapy," in *Studies in Philosophy and the History of Philosophy*, John K. Ryan, ed. Washington, D.C., Catholic University of America Press, 1974.

Spiegelberg, Herbert, "Viktor Frankl: Phenomenology in Logotherapy and *Existenzanalyse*," in *Phenomenology in Psychology and Psychiatry*. Evanston, Illinois, Northwestern University Press, 1972.

Strunk, Orlo, "Religious Maturity and Viktor E. Frankl," in *Mature Religion*. New York and Nashville, Abingdon Press, 1965.

Tyrell, Bernard J., "Logotherapy and Christotherapy," in *Christotherapy: Healing through Enlightenment*. New York, The Seabury Press, 1975.

Vanderveldt, James H., and Robert P. Odenwald, "Existential Analysis," in *Psychiatry and Catholicism*. New York, McGraw-Hill, 1952.

Zavalloni, Roberto, "Human Freedom and Logotherapy," in *Self-Determination*. Chicago, Forum Books, 1962.

3. ARTICLES AND MISCELLANEOUS*

Ansbacher, Rowena R., "The Third Viennese School of Psychotherapy." *Journal of Individual Psychology*, XV (1959), 236–37.

Ballard, R. E., "An Empirical Investigation of Viktor Frankl's Concept of the Search for Meaning: A Pilot Study with a Sample of Tuberculosis Patients." Doctoral dissertation, Michigan State University, 1965.

Birnbaum, Ferdinand, "Frankl's Existential Psychology from the

* Denotes works appearing in *Psychotherapy and Existentialism: Selected Papers on Logotherapy*. New York: Washington Square Press; 1967.

Viewpoint of Individual Psychology." *Journal of Individual Psychology*, XVII (1961), 162–66.

Bordeleau, Louis-Gabriel, "La Relation entre les valeurs de choix vocationnel et les valeurs créatrices chez V. E. Frankl." Doctoral dissertation presented to the Department of Psychology, The University of Ottawa, 1971.

Bulka, Reuven P., "An Analysis of the Viability of Frankl's Logotherapeutic System as a Secular Theory." Thesis presented to the Department of Religious Studies of the University of Ottawa as partial fulfillment of the requirements for the degree of Master of Arts, 1969.

———, "Denominational Implications of the Religious Nature of Logotherapy." Thesis presented to the Department of Religious Studies of the University of Ottawa as partial fulfillment of the requirements for the degree of Doctor of Philosophy, 1971.

———, "Logotherapy and Judaism—Some Philosophical Comparisons." *Tradition*, XII (1972), 72–89.

———, "Logotherapy and Judaism." *Jewish Spectator*, XXXVII, No. 7 (Sept. 1972), 17–19.

———, "Death in Life—Talmudic and Logotherapeutic Affirmations." *Humanitas (Journal of the Institute of Man)*, X, No. 1 (Feb. 1974), 33–42.

———, "The Ecumenical Ingredient in Logotherapy." *Journal of Ecumenical Studies*, XI, No. 1 (Winter 1974), 13–24.

Burck, James Lester, "The Relevance of Viktor Frankl's 'Will to Meaning' for Preaching to Juvenile Delinquents." A Master of Theology thesis submitted to the Southern Baptist Theological Seminary, Louisville, Kentucky, 1966.

Calabrese, Edward James, "The Evolutionary Basis of Logotherapy." Dissertation, University of Massachusetts, 1974.

Cavanagh, Michael E., "The Relationship between Frankl's 'Will to Meaning' and the Discrepancy Between the Actual Self and the Ideal Self." Doctoral dissertation, University of Ottawa, 1966.

Crumbaugh, James C., "The Application of Logotherapy." *Journal of Existentialism*, V (1965), 403–12.

———, "Cross Validation of Purpose-in-Life Test Based on Frankl's Concepts." *Journal of Individual Psychology*, XXIV (1968), 74–81.

———, "Frankl's Logotherapy: A New Orientation in Counseling." *Journal of Religion and Health*, X (1971), 373–86.

———, "Changes in Frankl's existential vacuum as a measure of therapeutic outcome." *Newsletter for Research in Psychology*

(Veterans Administration Center, Bay Pines, Florida), Vol. 14, No. 2 (May 1972), 35–37.

——, "Frankl's Logotherapy: An Answer to the Crisis in Identity." *Newsletter of the Mississippi Personnel & Guidance Association,* IV, No. 2 (Oct. 1972), 3.

——, "Aging and Adjustment: The Applicability of Logotherapy and the Purpose-in-Life Test." *The Gerontologist,* XII (1972), 418–20.

—— and Leonard T. **Maholick,** "The Case for Frankl's 'Will to Meaning.'" *Journal of Existential Psychiatry,* IV (1963), 43–48.

——, "An Experimental Study in Existentialism: The Psychometric Approach to Frankl's Concept of *Noögenic Neurosis.*"* *Journal of Clinical Psychology,* XX (1964), 200–207.

——, Sister **Mary Raphael** and Raymond R. **Shrader,** "Frankl's Will to Meaning in a Religious Order" (delivered before Division 24, American Psychological Association, at the annual convention in San Francisco, August 30, 1968). *Journal of Clinical Psychology,* XXVI (1970), 206–207.

Dansart, Bernard, "Development of a Scale to Measure Attitudinal Values as Defined by Viktor Frankl." Dissertation, Northern Illinois University, De Kalb, 1974.

Dickson, Charles W., "Logotherapy and the Redemptive Encounter." *Dialogue,* Spring 1974, 110–14.

Duncan, Franklin D., "Logotherapy and the Pastoral Care of Physically Disabled Persons." A thesis in the Department of Psychology of Religion submitted to the faculty of the Graduate School of Theology in partial fulfillment of the requirements for the degree of Master of Theology at Southern Baptist Theological Seminary, Louisville, Kentucky, 1968.

Fabry, Joseph, "A Most Ingenious Paradox." *The Register-Leader of the Unitarian Universalist Association,* Vol. 149 (June 1967), 7–8.

—— and Max **Knight** (pseud. Peter Fabrizius), "Viktor Frankl's Logotherapy." *Delphian Quarterly,* XLVII, No. 3 (1964), 27–30.

——, "The Use of Humor in Therapy." *Delphian Quarterly,* XLVIII, No. 3 (1965), 22–36.

Forstmeyer, Annemarie von, "The Will to Meaning as a Prerequisite for Self-Actualization." Thesis presented to the faculty of California Western University, San Diego, in partial fulfillment of the requirements for the degree Master of Arts, 1968.

Fox, Douglas A., "Logotherapy and Religion." *Religion in Life,* XXXI (1965), 235–44.

Frankl, Viktor E., "Logos and Existence in Psychotherapy." *American Journal of Psychotherapy*, VII (1953), 8–15.

———, "Group Psychotherapeutic Experiences in a Concentration Camp"* (paper read before the Second International Congress of Psychotherapy, Leiden, Netherlands, Sept. 8, 1951). *Group Psychotherapy*, VII (1954), 81–90.

———, "The Concept of Man in Psychotherapy" (paper read before the Royal Society of Medicine, Section of Psychiatry, London, England, June 15, 1944). *Pastoral Psychology*, VI (1955), 16–26.

———, "From Psychotherapy to Logotherapy." *Pastoral Psychology*, VII (1956), 56–60.

———, "Guest Editorial." *Academy Reporter*, III, No. 5 (May 1958), 1–4.

———, "On Logotherapy and Existential Analysis" (paper read before the Association for the Advancement of Psychoanalysis, New York, April 17, 1957). *American Journal of Psychoanalysis*, XVIII (1958), 28–37.

———, "The Will to Meaning." *Journal of Pastoral Care*, XII (1958), 82–88.

———, "The Search for Meaning." *Saturday Review* (Sept. 13, 1958).

———, "The Spiritual Dimension in Existential Analysis and Logotherapy"* (paper read before the Fourth International Congress of Psychotherapy, Barcelona, Sept. 5, 1958). *Journal of Individual Psychology*, XV (1959), 157–65.

———, "Beyond Self-Actualization and Self-Expression" * (paper read before the Conference on Existential Psychotherapy, Chicago, Dec. 13, 1959). *Journal of Existential Psychiatry*, I (1960), 5–20.

———, "Paradoxical Intention: A Logotherapeutic Technique" * (paper read before the American Association for the Advancement of Psychotherapy, New York, Feb. 26, 1960). *American Journal of Psychotherapy*, XIV (1960), 520–35.

———, "Logotherapy and the Challenge of Suffering" * (paper read before the American Conference on Existential Psychotherapy, New York, Feb. 27, 1960). *Review of Existential Psychology and Psychiatry*, I (1961), 3–7.

———, "Religion and Existential Psychotherapy." *Gordon Review*, VI (1961), 2–10.

———, "Dynamics, Existence and Values." * *Journal of Existential Psychiatry*, II (1961), 5–16.

———, "Psychotherapy and Philosophy." *Philosophy Today*, V (1961), 59–64.

——, "Basic Concepts of Logotherapy," *Journal of Existential Psychiatry*, III (1962), 111–18.

——, "Psychiatry and Man's Quest for Meaning." * *Journal of Religion and Health*, I (1962), 93–103.

——, "Logotherapy and the Challenge of Suffering." *Pastoral Psychology*, XIII (1962), 25–28.

——, "The Will to Meaning." *Living Church*, CXLIV (June 24, 1962), 8–14.

——, "Angel as Much as Beast: Man Transcends Himself." *Unitarian Universalist Register-Leader*, CXLIV (Feb. 1963), 8–9.

——, "Existential Dynamics and Neurotic Escapism" * (paper read before the Conference on Existential Psychiatry, Toronto, May 6, 1962). *Journal of Existential Psychiatry*, IV (1963), 27–42.

——, "Existential Escapism." * *Motive*, XXIV (Jan.Feb. 1964), 11–14.

——, "The Will to Meaning" * (paper read before the Conference on Phenomenology, Lexington, April 4, 1963). *Christian Century*, LXXI (April 22, 1964), 515–17.

——, "In Steady Search for Meaning." *Liberal Dimension*, II, No. 2 (1964), 3–8.

——, "The Concept of Man in Logotherapy" (175th Anniversary Lecture, Georgetown University, Washington, D.C., February 27, 1964). *Journal of Existentialism*, VI (1965), 53–58.

——, "Logotherapy and Existential Analysis: A Review" (paper read before the Symposium on Logotherapy, 6th International Congress of Psychotherapy, London, August 26, 1964). *American Journal of Psychotherapy*, XX (1966), 252–60.

——, "Self-Transcendence As a Human Phenomenon." *Journal of Humanistic Psychology*, VI, No. 2 (Fall 1966), 97–106.

——, "What is Meant by Meaning?" *Journal of Existentialism*, VII, No. 25 (Fall 1966), 21–28.

——, "Time and Responsibility." *Existential Psychiatry*, I (1966), 361–66.

——, "Logotherapy and Existentialism." *Psychotherapy: Theory, Research and Practice*, IV, No. 3 (Aug. 1967), 138–42.

——, "What is a Man?" *Life Association News*, LXII, No. 9 (Sept. 1967), 151–57.

——, "Logotherapy." *The Israel Annals of Psychiatry and Related Disciplines*, VII (1967), 142–55.

——, "Experiences in a Concentration Camp." *Jewish Heritage*, XI (1968), 5–7.

——, "The Search for Meaning" (abstract from a series of lectures given at the Brandeis Institute in California). *Jewish Heritage,* XI (1968), 8–11.

——, "Eternity Is the Here and Now." *Pace,* V, No. 4 (April 1969), 2.

——, "Youth in Search for Meaning" (3rd Paul Dana Bartlett Memorial Lecture). *The Baker World (The Baker University Newsletter),* I, No. 4 (Jan. 1969), 2–5.

——, "The Cosmos and the Mind. (How Far Can We Go?) A Dialogue with Geoffrey Frost." *Pace,* V, No. 8 (Aug. 1969), 34–39.

——, Fore-Runner of Existential Psychiatry." *Journal of Individual Psychology,* XXVI (1970), 12.

——, "Entering the Human Dimension." *Attitude,* I (1970), 2–6.

——, "Determinism and Humanism." *Humanitas (Journal of the Institute of Man),* VII (1971), 23–36.

——, "The Feeling of Meaninglessness: A Challenge to Psychotherapy." *The American Journal of Psychoanalysis,* XXXII, No. 1 (1972), 85–89.

——, "Man in Search of Meaning." *Widening Horizons* (Rockford College), Vol. 8, No. 5, August 1972.

——, "Encounter: The Concept and Its Vulgarization." *The Journal of the American Academy of Psychoanalysis,* I, No. 1 (1973), 73–83.

——, "The Depersonalization of Sex." *Synthesis (The Realization of the Self),* I (Spring 1974), 7–11.

Gerz, Hans O., "The Treatment of the Phobic and the Obsessive-Compulsive Patient Using Paradoxical Intention sec. Viktor E. Frankl." * *Journal of Neuropsychiatry,* III, No. 6 (July-Aug. 1962), 375–87.

——, "Experience with the Logotherapeutic Technique of Paradoxical Intention in the Treatment of Phobic and Obsessive-Compulsive Patients" (paper read at the Symposium of Logotherapy at the 6th International Congress of Psychotherapy, London, England, August 1964). *American Journal of Psychiatry,* CXXIII, No. 5 (Nov. 1966), 548–53.

——, "Reply." *American Journal of Psychiatry,* CXXIII, No. 10 (April 1967), 1306.

Green, Herman H., "The 'Existential Vacuum' and the Pastoral Care of Elderly Widows in a Nursing Home," Master's Thesis, Southern Baptist Theological Seminary, Louisville, Kentucky, 1970.

Grollman, Earl A., "Viktor E. Frankl: A Bridge Between Psychiatry and Religion." *Conservative Judaism,* XIX, No. 1 (Fall 1964), 19–23.

———, "The Logotherapy of Viktor E. Frankl." *Judaism*, XIV (1965), 22–38.

Grossman, Nathan, "The Rabbi and the Doctor of the Soul." *Jewish Spectator*, XXXIV, No. 1 (Jan. 1969), 8–12.

Guldbrandsen, Francis Aloysius, "Some of the Pedagogical Implications in the Theoretical Work of Viktor Frankl in Existential Psychology: A Study in the Philosophic Foundations of Education." Doctoral dissertation, Michigan State University, 1972.

Hall, Mary Harrington, "A Conversation with Viktor Frankl of Vienna." *Psychology Today*, I, No. 9 (Feb. 1968), 56–63.

Harrington, Donald Szantho, "The View from the Existential Vacuum," *Academy Reporter*, IX, No. 9 (Dec. 1964), 1–4.

Havens, Leston L., "Paradoxical Intention." *Psychiatry & Social Science Review*, II (1968), 16–19.

Haworth, D. Swan, "Viktor Frankl." *Judaism*, XIV (1965), 351–352.

Henderson, J. T., "The Will to Meaning of Viktor Frankl as a meaningful factor of personality." Master's thesis, The University of Maryland, 1970.

Holmes, R. M., "Meaning and Responsibility: A Comparative Analysis of the Concept of the Responsible Self in Search of Meaning in the Thought of Viktor Frankl and H. Richard Niebuhr with Certain Implications for the Church's Ministry to the University." Doctoral dissertation, Pacific School of Religion, Berkeley, California, 1965.

———, "Alcoholics Anonymous as Group Logotherapy." *Pastoral Psychology*, XXI (1970), 30–36.

Hyman, William, "Practical Aspects of Logotherapy in Neurosurgery." *Existential Psychiatry*, VII (1969), 99–101.

Johnson, Paul E., "Logotherapy: A Corrective for Determinism." *Christian Advocate*, V (Nov. 23, 1961), 12–13.

———, "The Challenge of Logotherapy." *Journal of Religion and Health*, VII (1968), 122–30.

———, "Meet Doctor Frankl." *Adult Student*, XXIV (Oct. 1964), 8–10.

———, "The Meaning of Logotherapy." *Adult Student*, XXVI, No. 8 (April 1967), 4–5.

Jones, Elbert Whaley, "Nietzsche and Existential-Analysis." Dissertation in the Department of Philosophy submitted to the faculty of the Graduate School of Arts and Sciences in partial fulfillment of the requirements for the degree of Master of Arts, New York University, 1967.

Kaczanowski, Godfryd, "Frankl's Logotherapy." *American Journal of Psychiatry*, CXVII (1960), 563.

————, "Logotherapy—A New Psychotherapeutic Tool." *Psychosomatics*, Vol. 8 (May–June 1967), 158–61.

Klapper, Naomi, "On Being Human: A Comparative Study of Abraham J. Heschel and Viktor Frankl." Doctoral dissertation, Jewish Theological Seminary of America, New York, 1973.

Klitzke, Louis L., "Students in Emerging Africa: Humanistic Psychology and Logotherapy in Tanzania," *Journal of Humanistic Psychology*, IX (1969), 105–26.

Kosukegawa, Tsugio, "A Comparative Study of the Differences Between Christian Existence and Secular Existence, and of Their Existential Frustration." *Japanese Journal of Educational and Social Psychology*, VII, No. 2 (1968), 195–208.

Lapinsohn, Leonard I., "Relationship of the Logotherapeutic Concepts of Anticipatory Anxiety and Paradoxical Intention to the Neurophysiological Theory of Induction." *Behavioral Neuropsychiatry*, III, No. 3–4 (1971), 12–14 and 24.

Leslie, Robert C., "Viktor E. Frankl's New Concept of Man." *Motive*, XXII (1962), 16–19.

Marrer, Robert F., "Existential-Phenomenological Foundations in Logotherapy Applicable to Counseling." Dissertation, Ohio University, 1972.

Maslow, A. H., "Comments on Dr. Frankl's Paper." *Journal of Humanistic Psychology*, VI (1966), 107–12.

"Meaning in Life." *Time* (Feb. 2, 1968), 38–40.

Meier, Augustine, "Frankl's 'Will to Meaning' as Measured by the Purpose in Life Test in Relation to Age and Sex Differences." Dissertation presented to The University of Ottawa, 1973.

Muilenberg, Don T., "Meaning in Life: Its Significance in Psychotherapy." A dissertation presented to the faculty of the Graduate School, University of Missouri, 1968.

Müller-Hegemann, D., "Methodological Approaches in Psychotherapy: Current Concepts in East Germany." *American Journal of Psychotherapy*, XVII (1963), 554–68.

Murphy, Leonard: "Extent of Purpose-in-Life and Four Frankl-Proposed Life Objectives." Doctoral dissertation in Department of Psychology, The University of Ottawa, 1967.

Murphy, Maribeth L., "Viktor Frankl: The New Phenomenology of Meaning." *The U.S.I.U. Doctoral Society Journal*, III, No. 2 (June 1970), 1–10, and IV, No. 1 (Winter 1970–71), 45–46.

Newton, Joseph R., "Therapeutic Paradoxes, Paradoxical Intentions, and Negative Practice." *American Journal of Psychotherapy*, XXII (1968), 68–81.

O'Connell, Walter E., "Viktor Frankl, the Adlerian?" *Psychiatric Spectator*, Vol. VI, No. 11 (1970), 13–14.

———, "Frankl, Adler, and Spirituality." *Journal of Religion and Health*, XI (1972), 134–38.

"Originator of Logotherapy Discusses Its Basic Premises" (interview). *Roche Report: Frontiers of Clinical Psychiatry*, Vol. 5, No. 1 (Jan. 1, 1968), 5–6.

Pervin, Lawrence A., "Existentialism, Psychology, and Psychotherapy." *American Psychologist*, XV (1960), 305–309.

Polak, Paul, "Frankl's Existential Analysis." *American Journal of Psychotherapy*, III (1949), 517–22.

Richmond, Bert O., Robert L. Mason and Virginia Smith, "Existential Frustration and Anomie." *Journal of Women's Deans and Counselors*, Spring 1969.

Rowland, Stanley J., Jr., "Viktor Frankl and the Will to Meaning." *Christian Century*, LXXIX (June 6, 1962), 722–24.

Ruggiero, Vincent R., "Concentration Camps Were His Laboratory." *The Sign*, XLVII (Dec. 1967), 13–15.

Sahakian, William S., and Barbara Jacquelyn Sahakian, "Logotherapy as a Personality Theory." *The Israel Annals of Psychiatry and Related Disciplines*, X (1972), 230–44.

Sargent, George Andrew, "Job Satisfaction, Job Involvement and Purpose in Life: A Study of Work and Frankl's Will to Meaning." Thesis presented to the faculty of the United States International University in partial fulfillment of the requirements for the degree Master of Arts, 1971.

———, "Motivation and Meaning: Frankl's Logotherapy in the Work Situation." Dissertation, United States International University, 1973.

Schachter, Stanley J., "Bettelheim and Frankl: Contradicting Views of the Holocaust." *Reconstructionist*, XXVI, No. 20 (Feb. 10, 1961), 6–11.

Solyom, L., J. Garza-Perez, B. L. Ledwidge and C. Solyom, "Paradoxical Intention in the Treatment of Obsessive Thoughts: A Pilot Study." *Comprehensive Psychiatry*, Vol. 13, No. 3 (May 1972), 291–97.

"The Doctor and the Soul: Dr. Viktor Frankl," *Harvard Medical Alumni Bulletin*, XXXVI, No. 1 (Fall 1961), 8.

"The Father of Logotherapy." *Existential Psychiatry*, Vol. I (1967), 439.

Turner, R. H., "Comment on Dr. Frankl's Paper." *Journal of Existential Psychiatry*, I (1960), 21–23.

Victor, Ralph G., and Carolyn M. Krug, " 'Paradoxical Intention' in the Treatment of Compulsive Gambling." *American Journal of Psychotherapy*, XXI, No. 4 (Oct. 1967), 808–14.

"Viktor Frankl." *The Colby Alumnus*, LI (Spring 1962), 5.

Waugh, Robert J. L., "Paradoxical Intention." *American Journal of Psychiatry*, Vol. 123, No. 10 (April 1967), 1305–1306.

Weiss, M. David, "Frankl's Approach to the Mentally Ill." *Association of Mental Hospital Chaplains' Newsletter*, Fall 1962, 39–42.

Weisskopf-Joelson, Edith, "Some Comments on a Viennese School of Psychiatry." *Journal of Abnormal and Social Psychology*, LI (1955), 701–703.

———, "Logotherapy and Existential Analysis." *Acta Psychotherapeutica*, VI (1958), 193–204.

———, "Paranoia and the Will-to-Meaning." *Existential Psychiatry*, I (1966), 316–20.

———, "Some Suggestions Concerning the Concept of Awareness." *Psychotherapy: Theory, Research and Practice*, VIII (1971), 2–7.

Yeates, J. W., "The Educational Implications of the Logotherapy of Viktor E. Frankl." Doctoral dissertation, University of Mississippi, 1968.

4. FILMS, RECORDS AND TAPES

Frankl, Viktor E., "Logotherapy," a film produced by the Department of Psychiatry, Neurology, and Behavioral Sciences, University of Oklahoma Medical School.

———, "Frankl and the Search for Meaning," a film produced by Psychological Films, 1215 East Chapman Ave., Orange, California 92666.

———, "Some Clinical Aspects of Logotherapy. Paper read before the Anderson County Medical Society in South Carolina," "Man in Search of Meaning. Address given to the Annual Meeting of the Anderson County Mental Health Association in South Carolina," and "Man's Search for Ultimate Meaning. Lecture given at the Peachtree Road Methodist Church in Atlanta, Georgia," videotapes cleared for television upon request from WGTV, the University of Georgia, Athens, Georgia 30601.

———, "Meaning and Purpose in Human Experience," a videotape produced by Rockland Community College. Rental or purchase through the Director of Library Services, 145 College Road, Suffern, New York 10901.

———, "Education and the Search for Meaning. An Interview by Professor William Blair Gould of Bradley University," a videotape produced by Bradley University Television. Available by request from Bradley University, Peoria, Illinois 61606 ($25 handling charges for usage).

———, "Youth in Search for Meaning. The Third Paul Dana Bartlett Memorial Lecture," a videotape produced by KNBU and cleared for television upon request from President James Edward Doty, Baker University, Baldwin City, Kansas 66006.

———, "Clinical Aspects of Logotherapy," a videotaped lecture. Replay available by arrangement with Medical Illustration Services, Veterans Administration Hospital, 3801 Miranda Avenue, Palo Alto, California 94304.

———, "Logotherapy," a videotaped lecture. Available for rental or purchase from Educational Television, University of California School of Medicine, Department of Psychiatry, Langley Porter Neuropsychiatric Institute, 3rd Avenue and Parnassus Avenue, San Francisco, California 94112.

———, "Logotherapy Workshop," a videotaped lecture. Available for rental or purchase from Middle Tennessee State University, Learning Resource Center, Murfreesboro, Tennessee 37130.

———, "The Rehumanization of Psychotherapy. A Workshop Sponsored by the Division of Psychotherapy of the American Psychological Association," a videotape. Address inquiries concerning availability to Division of Psychotherapy, American Psychological Association, 1200 Seventeenth Street, N.W., Washington, D.C. 20036.

———, "Youth in Search of Meaning," a videotape produced by the Youth Corps and Metro Cable Television. Contact: Youth Corps, 56 Bond Street, Toronto, Ontario M5B 1X2, Canada.

———, "Man in Search of Meaning," a film interview with Jim Corey of CFTO Television in Toronto. Contact: Youth Corps, 56 Bond Street, Toronto, Ontario M5B 1X2, Canada.

———, "Human Freedom and Meaning in Life" and "Self-Transcendence—Therapeutic Agent in Sexual Neurosis," videotapes. Copies of the tapes can be ordered for a service fee. Address inquiries to the Manager, Learning Resource Distribution Center, United States International University, San Diego, California 92131.

———, "Three Lectures on Logotherapy," given at the Brandeis Institute, Brandeis, California 93064. Long-playing records.

———, "Man in Search of Meaning: Two Dialogues," "Self-Transcendence: The Motivational Theory of Logotherapy," "What Is Meant by Meaning?" and "Logotherapy and Existentialism," audiotapes produced by Sound Seminars, College Division, McGraw-Hill Book Company, P. O. Box 402, Hightstown, New Jersey 08520.

———, "The Student's Search for Meaning," an audiotape produced by WGTV, the University of Georgia, Athens, Georgia 30601.

———, "The Existential Vacuum" ("Existential Frustration as a Challenge to Psychiatry," "Logotherapy as a Concept of Man," "Logotherapy as a Philosophy of Life"), tapes produced by Argus Communications, 3505 North Ashland Avenue, Chicago, Illinois 60657.

———, "The Existential Vacuum: A Challenge to Psychiatry. Address given at The Unitarian Church, San Francisco, California, October 13, 1969." A tape produced by Big Sur Recordings, 2015 Bridgeway, Sausalito, California 94965.

———, "Meaninglessness: Today's Dilemma," an audiotape produced by Creative Resources, 4800 West Waco Drive, Waco, Texas 76703.

———, "Logotherapy Workshop," an audiotape produced by Middle Tennessee State University, Learning Resource Center, Murfreesboro, Tennessee 37130.

———, "Man's Search for Meaning. An Introduction to Logotherapy." Recording for the Blind, Inc., 215 East 58th Street, New York, New York 10022.

———, "Youth in Search of Meaning." Word Cassette Library, 4800 West Waco Drive, Waco, Texas 76703. $4.98.

——— and Huston Smith, "Value Dimensions in Teaching," a color television film produced by Hollywood Animators, Inc., for the California Junior College Association. Rental or purchase through Dr. Rex Wignall, Director, Chaffey College, Alta Loma, California 91701.

———, Robin W. Goodenough, Iver Hand, Oliver A. Phillips and Edith Weisskopf-Joelson, "Logotherapy: Theory and Practice. A Symposium Sponsored by the Division of Psychotherapy of the American Psychological Association," an audiotape. Address inquiries concerning availability to Division of Psychotherapy, American Psychological Association, 1200 Seventeenth Street, N.W., Washington, D.C. 20036.

Hale, Dr. William H., "An Interview with Viktor E. Frankl. With an Introduction by Dr. Edith Weisskopf-Joelson, Professor of Psychology at the University of Georgia," a videotape cleared for television upon request from WGTV, the University of Georgia, Athens, Georgia 30601.

Murray, Dr. Edward L., and Dr. Rolf von Eckartsberg, A Discussion with Dr. Viktor E. Frankl on "Logotherapy: Theory and Applied" conducted by two members of the Duquesne University Graduate School of Psychology, filmed July 25, 1972. Available for rental, fee $15. Mail request to Chairman, Department of Psychology, Duquesne University, Pittsburgh, Pennsylvania 15219.

"The Humanistic Revolution: Pioneers in Perspective," interviews with leading humanistic psychologists: Abraham Maslow, Gardner Murphy, Carl Rogers, Rollo May, Paul Tillich, Frederick Perls, Viktor Frankl, Alan Watts. Psychological Films, 1215 East Chapman Ave., Orange, California 92666. Sale $250; rental $20.

5. RECENT WORKS

Downing, Lester N., "Logotherapy," in *Counseling Theories and Techniques*. Chicago, Nelson-Hall, 1975.

Frankl, Viktor E., "Man's Search for Ultimate Meaning," in *Sacred Tradition and Psychotherapy*, Jacob Needleman, ed. (in preparation).

———, "Paradoxical Intention and Dereflection." *Psychotherapy: Theory, Research and Practice* (in press).

Sahakian, William S., "Logotherapy: The Will to Meaning," in *History and Systems of Psychology*. New York, John Wiley & Sons, Inc., 1975.

Index

About the Author

Viktor E. Frankl, M.D., Ph.D., is professor of neurology and psychiatry at the University of Vienna Medical School and professor of logotherapy at the United States International University (San Diego). He is the originator of what has come to be called the Third Viennese School of Psychotherapy (after Freud's psychoanalysis and Adler's individual psychology)—the school of logotherapy.

Dr. Frankl is the author of twenty books that have been translated into fourteen languages, including Japanese and Chinese. The American edition of his book *Man's Search for Meaning* has thus far sold over one and a half million copies. Gordon W. Allport in his preface to this book calls it "an introduction to the most significant psychological movement of our day." Dr. Frankl's first article was published in 1924 in the *International Journal of Psychoanalysis* at the invitation of Sigmund Freud.

Dr. Frankl has been a visiting professor at Harvard, Southern Methodist, Stanford and Duquesne Universities. Honorary Doctoral degrees have been conferred upon him by Loyola University (Chicago), Edgecliff College and Rockford College. Dr. Frankl has been a guest lecturer on 134 campuses in America and has also lectured in Australia, Asia and Africa. He is president of the Austrian Medical Society of Psychotherapy.